D0842546

JONAS SALK

A LERNER BIOGRAPHY

JONAS SALK
Conquering Polio

Stephanie Sammartino McPherson
with a Foreword by Darrell Salk, M.D.

Lerner Publications Company /Minneapolis

To my parents, Angelo and Marion Sammartino,
who had the wisdom to make me a Polio Pioneer;
to the memory of my mother-in-law, Marie McPherson,
who unfailingly gave her time and effort to the March of Dimes;
and to my husband, Richard,
whose constant good humor and encouragement keep me going

Copyright © 2002 by Stephanie Sammartino McPherson

All rights reserved. International copyright secured. No part of this book may be reproduced, stored in a retrieval system, or transmitted in any form or by any means—electronic, mechanical, photocopying, recording, or otherwise—without the prior written permission of Lerner Publications Company, except for the inclusion of brief quotations in an acknowledged review.

Lerner Publications Company
A division of Lerner Publishing Group
241 First Avenue North
Minneapolis, Minnesota 55401 U.S.A.

Website address: www.lernerbooks.com

Library of Congress Cataloging-in-Publication Data

McPherson, Stephanie Sammartino   *T 51182*
    Jonas Salk : conquering polio / by Stephanie Sammartino McPherson.
            p.   cm. — (A Lerner biography)
        Includes bibliographical references and index.
        ISBN: 0–8225–4964–6 (lib. bdg. : alk. paper)
        1. Salk, Jonas, 1914–1995—Juvenile literature. 2. Virologists—United States—Biography—Juvenile Literature. 3. Poliomyelitis vaccine—United States—Juvenile literature. [1. Salk, Jonas, 1914–1995. 2. Scientists. 3. Poliomyelitis vaccine.] I. Title. II. Series.
    QR31.S25 M376 2002
    610'.92—dc21   2001000849

Manufactured in the United States of America
1 2 3 4 5 6 – JR – 07 06 05 04 03 02

PRESCOTT, ARIZONA 86305

Contents

$18.95

Follett

3-25-08

Foreword

It always seemed a little silly to me how my father took special note when April 12 came around every year. I remembered the day in 1955 when the results of the field trial of the killed poliovirus vaccine were announced. I was eight years old. It was pretty exciting, with all the activity and the newspaper and television reporters, but I didn't really understand the impact of what was happening. People seemed pleased with something my father had done, which made sense to me because, after all, he was *my* father—I thought he was pretty special, anyway.

I was young enough that I do not remember life changing in the United States after the polio vaccine was introduced, but it certainly did. Parents felt a great release from fear. Almost every adult in the United States had experienced the anxiety of the summer polio season, and almost everyone had contributed in some way to the search for a vaccine. Tens of thousands of people volunteered time and effort to the National Foundation for Infantile Paralysis. Millions sent dimes and dollars to the "March of Dimes." On April 12, 1955, there was a sense of celebration and relief. Summers needed no longer to be a time of fear.

Only after I had become a physician myself did I begin to understand the significance of what had happened during those early years of my life. New frontiers had been crossed in public health and medicine, in scientific principles and charitable giving, in drug manufacturing and government regulation.

A group of middle school students recently asked me what kind of man my father was. I told them he was an inveterate optimist; he always believed that good things would prevail, especially if one worked hard for them. He was admired and loved by patients, friends, and coworkers for his gentleness and grace. He was a highly moral person and held tenaciously to ideas and concepts that he believed to be correct. Because of this, and because his ideas ran counter to accepted scientific beliefs, he was viewed by some colleagues as stubborn and standoffish. Because he would make intuitive leaps that some scientists felt were not adequately grounded, some never accepted his ideas, even after he went back and carefully supported them with observation and experiment.

Much to his dismay, he received a great deal of attention from the public and the news media. His greatest desire in those days was to "get back to the laboratory" to continue his research, but it was very difficult. The changes in his life that started on that April day in 1955 were simply too profound. Overnight, "Dr. Salk" became a folk hero. He had to adapt and learn new ways to do what made his heart leap and help make the world a better place.

The story of the development of effective vaccines against paralytic poliomyelitis is a fascinating and exciting one. Stephanie Sammartino McPherson has made a great effort to understand and describe the science accurately. More than that, she has recognized and presented the personal side of my father's story in a balanced and careful way. She has avoided the usual approach that tells the story as "a race to a vaccine" and "a controversy between scientists." This biography tells the full story, not just the story of newspaper headlines.

Darrell Salk, M.D.
February 23, 2001

7

Jonas Salk poses with his parents, Dora and Daniel, in 1918.

ONE

His Own Way

1914–1934

Four-year-old Jonas Salk stared down the street at a child with splints strapped to her legs. He was puzzled. In spite of the splints' sturdy support, the little girl needed help to stand. Walking required tremendous effort. More and more often, Jonas noticed crippled children on the sidewalks of his neighborhood in New York City.

Jonas looked down at his own strong, thin legs. He could run and jump and climb the stairs to his family's apartment so easily. What had happened to the other children? Could it happen to Jonas himself? Surely his parents wouldn't let it.

Of course, Dora and Daniel Salk were anxious to do everything possible to protect their son from polio. But so little was known about the crippling, sometimes fatal disease. Some people believed cats and dogs spread polio. Others thought that dirty living conditions played a role in causing the disease. Although several respected health officials disagreed, the *New York Times* urged people in crowded apartment buildings to keep their kitchens and bathrooms clean. Maybe that would keep the dreadful disease from spreading.

Even without this last advice, Dora Salk would have kept a spotless home. A determined and energetic woman, she had come to the United States from Russia when she was only twelve years old. Her family wanted to escape the violent pogroms of the late 1800s in which whole neighborhoods of Jews were attacked and their property confiscated or destroyed. Although Jonas's father had been born in New York, his parents had also come from Russia, looking for freedom to practice their Jewish faith.

Daniel Salk worked hard, designing and making lace collars for blouses. He had little education but was so talented that friends and customers said he had "golden hands." Jonas's mother had also been in the clothing business after coming to America. By the age of sixteen, she had supervised a factory of fifty garment workers. Even so, there wasn't much money for extras. The Salks couldn't afford to send their son away from the city during polio epidemics as many wealthier people did.

Born October 28, 1914, Jonas wasn't even two years old when the epidemic of 1916 struck. Thousands of children in New York City developed polio that summer. In every neighborhood, quarantine signs warned healthy people away from homes where people lay ill. A total of 217 new cases were reported on the worst day of all.

Dora and Daniel Salk were lucky. Jonas stayed healthy throughout those long, terrible months. Now, at four years old, he was a curious, active youngster—old enough, his parents felt, to attend New York City's Armistice Day parade. World War I had just ended, and all over the country people were celebrating with parades and festivities. Hemmed in by the jostling crowds, Daniel held Jonas high on his shoulders to see the shiny brass bands and the soldiers troop by. The music, the flags, and the marching soldiers would have been exciting to almost any little boy. But once again, Jonas was puzzled. Some of the soldiers limped painfully on crutches. Others couldn't walk at all. Still other veterans were bandaged or held their arms at odd, useless angles. What had happened to them, Jonas wondered? He was much too young to understand what war was really about. But he did know when people had been hurt. Whenever he thought about the parade, he remembered the injured soldiers.

Crowds jam the streets of New York to watch the Armistice Day parade in 1918.

Jonas never forgot anything that confused or bothered him. He was a serious little boy who listened carefully to all his parents' rules and sayings. "The early bird gets the worm," Dora Salk might remind him. Or "God helps him who helps himself." At a very young age, Jonas knew what these sayings meant. He was supposed to get good grades and keep his room neat. He was supposed to be respectful to his parents and to read lots of books—as long as they didn't have pictures. Dora Salk considered books with pictures too silly for her bright son to bother reading. She was more concerned with his future success than his everyday fun. When baby Herman was born, five-year-old Jonas was also expected to be

Jonas, right, *plays with one of his cousins.*

a model brother. Dutifully he kept quiet while the baby slept, helped his mother with simple chores, and shared his toys as Herman got older.

In school as well as at home, Jonas's training and self-discipline set him apart. Slim, dark haired, and wearing short knickers, Jonas looked young but acted much more grown-up than his classmates. He never got into trouble, and he had little time for jokes or games. But Jonas was friendly and loyal. He might not stand out in a crowd, but he was a great person to know—someone always willing to listen or willing to stand by a friend.

Relatives and family friends were as impressed as Jonas's classmates were. Aunts, uncles, and swarms of cousins often gathered in the Salks' small apartment. They listened carefully to Jonas's words and the ideas that he shared from his books. "Even as a kid, when Jonas said something, you could put it in the bank," a relative said.

But Jonas didn't talk much at family gatherings. He would much rather read than share news around the kitchen table. One cousin, Helen Press, thought he spent entirely too much time alone. Sometimes she couldn't resist seeking him out for a joke or a good-natured tease.

Jonas never knew what to expect from Helen. She seemed willing to make fun of almost everything. "You're outrageous!" he often exploded, but his eyes sparkled. No one could make him laugh the way Helen did.

Even with Helen distracting him, Jonas always got his schoolwork done. In fact, he learned so quickly that he skipped several grades. When he was only twelve years old, he was ready for high school. But not just any high school would do for Dora and Daniel's son. They wanted him to go to Townsend Harris High School, a highly selective, three-year magnet school. Like a magnet attracts iron, the school was supposed to attract the brightest boys in New York City.

When Jonas was admitted to the school, his parents were delighted but not surprised. Although he would be one of the youngest students, Dora and Daniel still expected him to make top grades. Jonas, who was as ambitious as they were, didn't disappoint them.

Each afternoon after school, Jonas hurried home to his busy, immigrant neighborhood filled with the laughter and noise of children playing. After a few brief greetings, he entered his family's apartment instead of joining the games. Between homework assignments, Jonas helped take care of seven-year-old Herman and his new baby brother, Lee. Herman was a much livelier child than Jonas and liked to talk his big brother into playing stickball with him in the street.

Jonas never minded doing things with his brothers. But he was five years older than Herman, and sometimes he longed for a little free time on his own. There was little variety in his daily routine, and there were so many rules. "Someday I shall grow up and do something in my own way, without anyone telling me how," he promised himself. Just imagining it made Jonas long to grow up!

Compared to most children, Jonas did grow up quickly. He knew how to take care of himself and his brothers. He had grown-up dreams about what he wanted to do with his life. Instead of exploring the neighborhood, he found his greatest adventures in books. As a high school student, he enjoyed reading philosophy and literature. He especially liked the writings of Ralph Waldo Emerson and Henry David Thoreau. Emerson and Thoreau loved nature and had a strong faith in the power of the human mind. Already, Jonas shared their beliefs. Abraham Lincoln's writings also appealed

Left to right:
*Dora, Herman,
Daniel, Jonas,
and Lee Salk*

to Jonas because of their emphasis on equality and freedom. He could see for himself that even in the 1920s, people weren't treated equally. Jonas could think of many instances of discrimination against Jews. That's why Moses was as big a hero to him as Lincoln. Lincoln had freed the American slaves, and Moses had led the Jews out of captivity in Egypt.

The day after Jonas's fifteenth birthday, the stock market crashed. The Great Depression began—a time of intense financial hardship all over the United States. Many people lost their jobs and couldn't afford to buy food or pay the rent. Parents struggled to keep their families together and feed their children. Goods became scarce, and people stood in long lines just to buy bread.

The Salk family was more fortunate than many. Although fewer people could afford to buy the lace-trimmed blouses that Daniel Salk designed, there was enough money for food and other necessities. But Jonas was very sensitive to other people's suffering. The plight of hungry children and of adults desperate to find jobs was never far from his mind. Life wasn't fair, Jonas realized. It wasn't right for people to work hard only to see their livelihoods snatched away and their children's futures jeopardized.

Could anything be done to change things—to stop injustice and to create a prosperous society with enough jobs for everyone? A lawyer could surely do something, Jonas thought. Ever since he began high school, he had been thinking about what he would like to be someday. As a lawyer, he might be able to tackle some of the country's pressing social problems and help make life better for everyone.

Jonas's waiting to grow up was nearly over. At almost sixteen years old, he was ready to enter the City College of New York and eager to learn everything. Since he'd had little chance to study science in high school, he decided to take a chemistry course. He was curious to see what it was all about.

Soon Jonas found himself fascinated by the way atoms and molecules bound together to form chemical compounds. But something else attracted him to science too. Scientists asked their own questions and devised their own experiments. They discovered things no one had known before. Enthusiastically, Jonas rearranged his schedule to cram in as many science courses as he could. He especially loved biology, the study of living things. More and more, Jonas wondered if his real future lay in science.

While Jonas was deciding what to be, he had many talks with his parents. Trying to picture her son as a lawyer, Dora Salk jokingly remarked that if Jonas couldn't win an argument with her, how could he become a lawyer? Even Jonas couldn't answer that question!

It was the questions Jonas might answer someday that excited him when he thought about his future—questions about what caused disease and how illnesses affected society. By the time he graduated from college in 1934, his mind was made up. He was going to become a doctor.

At Jonas's admissions interview for New York University's College of Medicine, he explained that he didn't want to practice medicine. He wanted to do medical research. Surprised, the doctor interviewing him pointed out that a research doctor didn't make as much money as a doctor who treated patients. "There's more to life than money," Jonas replied. Already he was beginning to do things his own way.

Jonas graduated from City College in 1934 at the age of nineteen.

TWO

Medical Mystery
1934–1942

Although Jonas wasn't worried about earning a big salary, money was important when the time came to enroll in medical school. Jonas's parents scrimped and saved one thousand dollars to pay for his first year. Nineteen-year-old Jonas was determined to pay them back by being one of the top students in his class. It was the only return Daniel and Dora Salk wanted.

Jonas wanted to learn everything about medicine—even things that are not usually taught in medical school. By the end of his freshman year, his teachers had noticed his passion for research. One professor, Dr. R. Keith Cannan, suggested that he take some time off to study chemistry with him in greater depth. Jonas was one of the youngest in his class. He had nothing to lose by taking time off after his first year and everything to gain in terms of knowledge. Eagerly he agreed.

As Jonas began his year of study, a major medical story was unfolding. Two research doctors, Maurice Brodie of New York University and John Kolmer of Temple University, had independently developed polio vaccines. Made from the poliovirus itself, these preparations were intended to keep people from getting the disease. Each vaccine had been tested on children about the time that Jonas had started medical school. People hoped the vaccines would end the epidemics that had claimed thousands of victims almost every summer since Jonas's childhood.

But something went terribly wrong. In spite of both doctors' careful work, several children had contracted polio after their shots. By this time, investigators were trying to determine if the shots had caused the polio or if it was just a coincidence. Finally it was determined that the vaccines were ineffective as well as unsafe. Jonas felt badly for the sick children and for the doctors who had done their best and failed.

By September 1936, Jonas was back in medical school, eager to resume his studies. His classmates welcomed the pleasant, cheerful student, but sometimes they found him a little reserved. Jonas genuinely liked people, but he wasn't ready to share all his dreams and concerns. A part of his mind was always thinking about medicine, and he knew his classmates didn't want to discuss their courses *all* the time. Even at social events, Jonas spent much of his time thinking. Because he didn't know many young women, he often took his cousin Helen to medical school dances. Helen, who liked parties, was disappointed when he would seclude himself in a corner. With her usual blend of humor and determination, she would coax him onto the dance floor.

Jonas had good reason to be preoccupied during his second year as a medical student. In a small way, he was already trying to change research methods. His experiments with streptococcus bacteria, which caused serious throat infections, were routine. But he often thought about how hard it was to separate the bacteria from the medium in which they were grown. Maybe if he chilled the medium, the bacteria would collect together more easily. It was worth a try.

After some contradictory results, Jonas discovered that colder temperatures weren't the answer after all. It was the *way* he had chilled the medium that made a difference. Jonas had packed calcium chloride around the medium to help freeze it. When the chemical leaked into the medium, it turned into calcium phosphate, and the bacteria separated out easily. Calcium phosphate was the answer! The finding was so important that Jonas wrote it up as a scientific paper. He became a published author while he was still in medical school.

As a budding scientist, Jonas questioned everything in the laboratory. In the classroom, however, he was supposed to accept what his teachers told him. Sometimes this was hard. One spring day in 1937, Jonas listened intently as his professor discussed viruses—microscopic particles that infected living cells, then reproduced. In the process, the viruses destroyed the cells and caused diseases such as polio, influenza, or the common cold. The teacher was talking about how to prevent this from happening.

Jonas was intrigued by the concept of immunization, a way to stimulate the body's immune system to fight disease. Healthy people could be injected with a vaccine that contained a weakened form of a virus. This weakened virus wouldn't be strong enough to cause the disease, but it could trigger the body to make tiny proteins called antibodies to attack or kill the virus particles. After receiving a shot, or immunization, a person exposed to the same virus again would not get sick.

Then the teacher said something that really startled Jonas. In order to immunize a person, the virus in the vaccine had to be alive. By this, the teacher meant that the virus had to be able to reproduce itself in a living cell. Killed viruses—viruses specially treated to become harmless and unable to reproduce in cells—would not stimulate the body to produce the antibodies needed to prevent a person from getting the disease.

Jonas's thoughts raced back to the previous day's lecture. The teacher had said that toxins, or poisons, from bacteria could be chemically rendered into harmless toxoids and used to make a vaccine. The discrepancy glared at Jonas. "Something's wrong here," he thought. "Both statements can't be true."

Jonas knew that in some ways bacteria were very different from viruses. Larger and more complex than viruses, bacteria could live independently and reproduce outside of other organisms. This was not true of viruses. In spite of the differences, Jonas knew instinctively that the basic principles of immunization should hold true for both kinds of "germs." If chemically treated, harmless toxoids could cause immunity, why couldn't chemically treated, harmless viruses do the same thing? Jonas was so excited by his sudden insight that he couldn't stop thinking about it.

But Jonas wasn't ready to challenge his professor, and eventually he had to turn his thoughts in other directions. He was busy with his other classes and with lining up summer jobs. After his second year of medical school, he spent the summer as a lab worker in Woods Hole, Massachusetts. This quiet, seaside community, so different from bustling New York City, delighted Jonas. He enjoyed long walks on the beach and the small town friendliness.

Soon Jonas met a young woman named Donna Lindsay who was vacationing in Woods Hole. Jonas and Donna had a great deal in common. When Jonas talked about the injustice he'd seen in the world, Donna spoke of her own sense of fairness and desire to help others. Jonas liked sharing ideas with this intelligent, beautiful, and caring woman. He might be a bit cautious with his classmates, but with Donna he was relaxed and open. Best of all, Donna, who planned to be a social worker, attended graduate school in New York City. When Jonas returned to medical school, he could continue to see her if he could only find time in his hectic schedule.

Jonas Salk and Donna Lindsay

No matter how busy he was, Jonas *made* time. Often he invited Donna to medical lectures that related to her interests in psychology and social work. Soon she became as familiar a face at Jonas's school as she was at her own. Within months the young couple became engaged. They planned to get married when Jonas graduated in a year and a half.

Meanwhile, a new professor came to the medical school to teach and do research on bacteria and viruses. This was a chance for Jonas to learn about the topics that fascinated him most of all. He went to see Dr. Thomas Francis in his lab. "I have some time to fill in—is there anything I can do?" he asked.

Dr. Francis was happy to accept such an energetic helper. He explained that he was experimenting with the influenza virus. He wanted to kill the virus by exposing it to ultraviolet light, then see if he could use it to make mice immune to influenza. Jonas had stumbled into the perfect position. He had found a professor studying the very same question that had perplexed him earlier in the classroom. Now maybe he'd find out whether a killed-virus vaccine was possible after all.

Dr. Francis put Jonas to work infecting mice with the influenza virus. Then Jonas had to kill the mice to get the virus out of their lungs. Clutching his unusual harvest in racks of test tubes, he hurried forty-two blocks to the Rockefeller Institute. Here he carefully aimed ultraviolet light at the virus to kill it. Next, Jonas helped Dr. Francis inject the killed virus into healthy mice to see if it could trigger immunity.

To their delight, Jonas and Dr. Francis found that the vaccinated mice were protected from influenza. Jonas's hunch in the classroom had proved correct. A killed-virus preparation could confer immunity.

This was an exciting time for Jonas. On June 8, 1939, he graduated from medical school. The very next day, Jonas and

Donna were married. They moved into a small apartment, and Jonas continued working with Dr. Francis. In March 1940, Dr. Jonas Salk entered a residency program at New York's Mount Sinai Hospital. He was one of a dozen new doctors selected for the program out of 250 applicants.

Jonas had no more time to test the killed-virus principle. For two years, he did what most doctors do—examine sick patients and determine what's wrong with them. After making his diagnosis, he would prescribe a treatment to make the patient well or at least improve her condition. Jonas was so skilled that he became something of a legend. One time an obviously ill man caught Jonas's attention in the emergency room. Carefully he watched as the patient made his way down a flight of stairs. The man's stooped posture and awkward movement told Jonas right away what he needed to know. The patient was suffering from kidney stones, a painful condition in which small hard masses block the tubes leading from the kidneys. Now Jonas knew how to help him.

Another time Jonas was assigned to a patient who had been admitted to the hospital unconscious. There was no way to ask any of the routine questions that would help make a diagnosis. But Jonas smelled a chemical compound called acetone on the patient's breath. The clue was all he needed. He correctly concluded that the patient had diabetes and started emergency treatment at once. After this incident, several impressed residents began teasing Jonas. Grinning, they asked if he would like to smell some of their patients.

The intellectual challenge of medicine excited Jonas, but his concern went far beyond his patients' medical complaints. He also cared about their feelings and anxieties. Attentive and kind, he was always willing to take a few extra minutes to reassure a nervous patient. Even when he did something as simple as remove an insect from a patient's ear, Jonas let his patients know that they mattered to him.

Being a resident left little time for a private life. Donna got around his demanding schedule by spending all the time she could at the hospital. Three or four times a week, she joined Jonas for dinner at the hospital cafeteria. She sat around in the lounge listening to the residents discuss medicine. When she wasn't at the hospital, Donna could usually be found at the Jewish Child Care Association where she worked. An evening spent with her husband at home was a rare treat.

The pressure on Jonas Salk as a resident was continual, intense, and exhausting. Occasionally tempers around him flared. But no matter what was happening, Jonas stayed focused and calm. One of the doctors he worked for called him the best resident in the hospital. "You told him to do something and it got done. It got done and so did a dozen things you hadn't thought of."

Jonas's fellow residents noticed. They elected him president of their group. "He was a fine clinician and an incredibly patient and responsive mentor," one of the residents said. "It was a joy to work for him."

But Jonas also knew when to challenge his superiors. It was the early 1940s. Although the United States hadn't entered the war in Europe yet, many Americans gave money to the Allies, the European nations that were fighting to defeat Hitler. Those who contributed to the Allied cause received a special button to wear. Nevertheless, hospital rules said that residents weren't allowed to wear anything extra on their uniforms. The hospital director became furious when he saw one young doctor wearing an Allied button and vented his anger directly at Jonas.

Politely, Jonas listened. He believed it was more important to express support for the Allied campaign than to worry about a uniform rule. Although Jonas was just as angry as the hospital director, he didn't show his temper. Instead he called a meeting of all the residents and took a vote on how they felt about the issue. After that, every resident in the hospital wore a button supporting the Allied cause. Faced with the residents' united front, hospital administrators quietly backed down.

It was clear that Jonas knew how to get his way in dealing with hospital officials. He knew how to set patients at ease and how to inspire other doctors. He would be a great practicing physician, his friends thought. And he would do much better financially than he would in a lab. But as Jonas approached the end of his residency, he began looking for research opportunities.

Why? his friends wanted to know.

"Why did Mozart compose music?" countered Jonas.

It wasn't easy, however, for Jonas to find the position he was looking for. Several research facilities rejected his application. Later he found out that at least one well-known researcher objected to having someone Jewish on the staff. By this time, the United States had entered World War II, and Thomas Francis had moved to the University of Michigan. Dr. Francis, Jonas's friend and mentor, was still working on a vaccine to prevent influenza. The government considered this vital research. By the end of World War I, more soldiers had died of influenza than in combat. Everyone was anxious to avoid a repeat epidemic during World War II. Here was an opportunity for Jonas Salk to pursue research and save lives. He accepted a job with his former professor and prepared to move to Ann Arbor, Michigan.

Left to right: *Herman, Lee, Donna, Dora, and Jonas in New York City in 1940*

ⓣⓗⓡⓔⓔ

Liberation

1942–1948

Leaving New York was a great adventure for Jonas and Donna. Instead of settling in Ann Arbor, they moved into an old farmhouse outside the town. For the first time, Jonas needed a car to get to work. On cold mornings, Jonas had to hand crank the motor in his second-hand car before the engine sputtered to life. But living in the country was worth the inconvenience. Like many other people during the war, the Salks planted a big victory garden. At night, Jonas fed sticks into the wood-burning stove to heat up the kitchen while Donna cooked supper on the electric range. In the winter, they ate the homegrown vegetables that Donna had canned.

Jonas Salk still worked long hours, but he didn't mind because his experiments were so fascinating. His mind was always leaping ahead to new questions, new possibilities. "I wanted to do independent work and I wanted to do it my way," Salk said.

Salk was so innovative that he sometimes frustrated Thomas Francis, head of the Army Influenza Commission.

"Damn it all, Salk," he once complained. "Why can't you do things the way everyone else does?" In spite of his impatience, however, Francis respected and trusted Salk. He also knew that "Salk's way" led to sound, practical results.

Salk had begun his new position by reviewing all the latest developments in his field. The work of George Hirst, a New York virologist, had been especially interesting. Hirst had discovered that the influenza virus caused red blood cells to stick together, or agglutinate. Fascinated, Salk decided to conduct his own experiments by adding the virus to blood samples in test tubes. Then he studied the size and number of the blood cell clumpings that were formed. Based on the clumps, Salk developed a method to measure antibodies in

Jonas, right, worked for Dr. Thomas Francis to develop an influenza vaccine.

the blood samples. As Salk measured antibodies, he made another discovery. The higher the level of antibodies in the
blood, the less likely a person was to get influenza, or flu.

As a virologist, Salk's job was to make a vaccine that would
boost antibodies against influenza to the highest possible level.
The task was challenging because there was more than one
kind of flu virus. The two main types of flu, called A and B, were
divided into over one hundred different strains. If a person had
antibodies to one strain, he could still get flu from another
strain. To complicate the matter even further, influenza viruses
constantly mutated, or developed into new strains. Salk needed
a vaccine that would protect against many strains of influenza.
The health of American soldiers depended on his work.

In 1943 Salk visited an army base to investigate an unusual illness that had broken out. Some doctors thought it was
a kind of pneumonia, but Salk soon discovered that the sick
men really had influenza. He did some quick, careful experiments and found that the Weiss strain of type A of the virus
was causing the soldiers' epidemic. The identification surprised Salk. He hadn't considered this particular strain a serious menace. It wasn't even included in the experimental
vaccine he was making with Dr. Francis. That meant men inoculated, or given a shot, with the vaccine could still become
ill from the Weiss strain.

Salk returned to Ann Arbor and talked it over with Dr.
Francis. They decided to include the Weiss strain in the next
batch of vaccine they made. "To avoid . . . the failures so often
ascribed to flu vaccines, you must cram your vaccine with
every strain you can lay hands on," Salk said. The next winter, the vaccine was tested on more than one thousand army
recruits. Other soldiers were used as controls—a group of
people who received no shots but were observed to see how

many got sick. The numbers told a convincing story. The men who had been inoculated had a seventy-five percent lower rate of influenza than the control group of men who had not received the vaccine. Salk and Francis were overjoyed.

Busy with experiments and tests and travel, Jonas had little spare time, but he cherished his quiet evenings at home. In 1944 Donna gave birth to their first child, a little boy named Peter. Jonas loved being a father. He wanted Peter to have a more relaxed childhood than his own, with lots of time for fun as well as schoolwork. But caught in the crunch of vital research, Jonas couldn't play with his son very much.

Peter was not quite two years old when his father prepared to go on another trip. World War II had ended, and American troops were being sent to occupy the defeated countries. Jonas was chosen to go to Germany to prevent an outbreak of influenza among the American soldiers. For this assignment, he was sworn into the army, given the temporary rank of major, and flown overseas. Although Donna worried about his safety so far from home, Jonas experienced no danger and enjoyed putting his work to practical use. Thanks to his efforts, thousands of soldiers were protected from influenza.

Salk had come a long way from the young resident who had entered Dr. Francis's lab. He'd made discoveries, tested his ideas, and helped to head a large-scale vaccination program. At thirty-three years old, he was as independent and ambitious as ever. It was time for another career move, Salk decided. He wanted a lab of his own.

Nearly two years passed before he got the chance he was waiting for. By that time, Peter was an active little boy of three, and Jonas and Donna had a second baby boy named Darrell. In the spring of 1947, Jonas took a quick trip to see what their

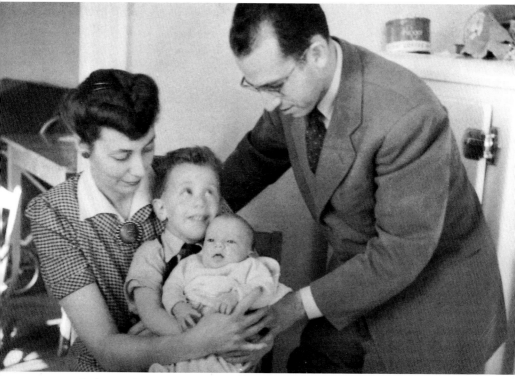

Left to right: *Donna, Peter, Darrell, and Jonas in the spring of 1947*

lives would be like in Pittsburgh, Pennsylvania, where he had a promising job offer.

At once, Jonas saw that the lab at the University of Pittsburgh was older and less convenient than his modern facility in Ann Arbor. The medical school at Pittsburgh did very little research. But there was lots of empty space in the Municipal Hospital where Jonas would be located. Eventually he might be able to expand. More importantly, the lab would be all his! He could chart his own course and create a strong research department. Walking through the Municipal Hospital, there wasn't any doubt in Jonas's mind. He would come to Pittsburgh.

His friends and colleagues in Ann Arbor thought he was making a big mistake. "What's in Pittsburgh, for heaven's sake?" a colleague exclaimed.

"I guess I fell in love," replied Jonas. He could hardly wait to start doing things his own way in his own lab. But Dr. Francis was certain Jonas would regret his decision. He promised Jonas that if things didn't work out his first year in Pittsburgh, Jonas could come back to his old job.

Jonas remembered that promise often during his first difficult months in the Pittsburgh lab. But when he drove home, life was as pleasant as it had been in Michigan. Jonas and Donna had grown to like rural living and wanted their sons to enjoy the countryside too. They found a home surrounded by fields and woods in the nearby suburb of Wexford. Once again, they planted an enormous garden. Often it was dark when Jonas arrived home. Pulling into the garage on cold nights, he would check the furnace of the neighbors who lived in the apartment above the garage. When fuel was low, he would shovel in some coal before he hurried indoors to greet Donna, Peter, and the baby.

In contrast to his happy family life, Salk's work situation was a severe disappointment. The hospital had given him a lab that was even smaller than he'd hoped. Worse still, the university hemmed him in with countless rules. Everything Salk did had to be approved by the director of virus research, a scientist who was more interested in plant viruses than in the human viruses Salk was studying. Salk couldn't even determine what to pay his secretary without discussing it with the director. "Bound and gagged," is the way he described his situation.

Salk badly needed more room and more freedom. As he continued his study of influenza viruses, he waged a quiet campaign for some of the unused hospital space. Even get-ting an extra closet or office was a big accomplishment. Salk didn't seriously consider returning to Ann Arbor, but he won-dered what he had gotten himself into.

Then a visitor came to talk to Jonas. Harry Weaver was the director of research of an organization called the National Foundation for Infantile Paralysis. Infantile paralysis was an-other term for polio. It was called "infantile" because most of its victims were children, though adults could also get polio. "Paralysis" referred to the crippling of the children and adults who'd had the disease. In 1946 more than 25,000 chil-dren had become ill with polio. Although this was a small percentage of the population, parents were terrified of the

In the 1940s, people all over the country were terrified of polio. Here, baseball hero Babe Ruth visits polio patients in New York.

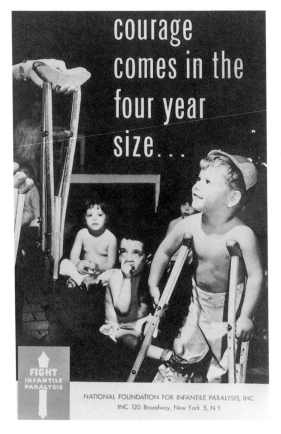

The March of Dimes raised money for the National Foundation for Infantile Paralysis to fight polio. Each year, a polio patient was chosen as the poster child.

strange, sometimes fatal disease. For years the National Foundation had been dedicated to trying to understand and eliminate polio.

Harry Weaver asked if Jonas Salk wanted to join the fight. He was looking for research doctors to help establish how many types of poliovirus there really were. Although there were many different strains, only three main types of the virus had been discovered. Most investigators believed there weren't any others, but their belief would have to be tested and retested. The work would be repetitious, boring, and would take several years. It would also require more space, equipment, and people than Salk had. But the National Foundation would pay for the needed improvements. When the project to type or classify the polioviruses was done, Salk could keep his new facilities and go on to other work. Maybe that work would involve a more exciting phase of polio research.

The opportunity was too good to pass up. "This was liberation." Jonas Salk readily agreed to join the team of doctors working to determine the number of poliovirus types.

Jonas was excited about beginning his research in typing poliovirus.

FOUR

Tracking Down the Virus
1948–1950

Hospital officials were happy to cooperate with the National Foundation for Infantile Paralysis. Although the official project wouldn't begin for a year, they allotted Salk more floor space at once. It was an exhilarating year for him as he recruited promising scientists for his staff and drew up floor plans for his new labs. He designed the equipment, selected office furniture, and even decided what type of plumbing he wanted and where the electrical outlets should go. From test tubes to monkey cages, nothing was too trivial for Salk to consider. He took a joyful pride in every last detail.

Jonas Salk was as considerate of people's feelings as he was careful about his lab. Part of his new space had once been the hospital auditorium. Some of the nurses and doctors were annoyed because now they had no place to hold dances and other special events. Acknowledging their disappointment, Jonas explained the importance of his work and thanked them for their sacrifice. When they realized what was at stake, the hospital staff felt better about giving up the auditorium. It was

Jonas visits the monkeys in the animal quarters at Municipal Hospital.

impossible not to like the kind and energetic doctor with the sympathetic ear and the ready smile. "Just plain downright nice," one nurse described him.

Jonas listened with that same sensitivity when Donna talked about Peter and Darrell's day. He understood four-year-old Peter's reluctance to sit still long enough for a haircut. Jonas, who decided to cut Peter's curly hair himself, gave his son special attention while he snipped away. Another thing that bothered Peter was shots. Whenever he had a sore throat or earache and needed a shot of an antibiotic, Jonas gave the injection while Peter was sleeping. Jonas was so careful that Peter hardly ever woke up!

Jonas wished he could spend much more time with his

sons. He drove Peter to nursery school but often didn't see him again until late in the evening. Sometimes Jonas came home exhausted. But Donna knew he was really more excited than tired. Besides studying flu viruses, he was bursting with ideas for the coming work on polio.

Jonas was already thinking of ways to improve the method for typing poliovirus. According to the standards set by the National Foundation, Salk would choose a type of the virus, say type I, and use it to infect a healthy monkey. After the monkey became sick and recovered, it would have antibodies to type I poliovirus in its blood. Then Salk would infect the monkey with an untyped poliovirus. If the monkey stayed well, it meant that the unknown virus must be type I because the monkey was already immune to that type. If the monkey got sick because it had no antibodies to the virus, the virus had to be type II or type III or an unknown type. If a virus made monkeys with antibodies to all three types of polio sick, it would be a type no one had discovered before. Neither Jonas Salk nor anyone else in the National Foundation expected to find a new type of poliovirus. But thousands of monkeys would be tested just to make sure.

Salk believed he could improve the long and costly method and was eager to hear what other scientists thought of his ideas. During his year of preparation for the typing project, Salk met with some of the top polio researchers at meetings convened by the National Foundation. One of his colleagues, Dr. Albert Sabin, who had been studying polio since 1931, believed firmly in traditional methods. At one meeting, Salk raised an issue that showed he took a different approach to virus typing from the one generally favored. Instead of the debate he hoped to inspire, he was stunned to hear his ideas dismissed. "Now, Dr. Salk, you should know better than to ask a question like that," said Dr. Sabin.

That was the end of the discussion. Salk felt frustrated and insulted. He hadn't realized how much even a respectful challenge would upset the established researchers. After that experience, the meetings became an ordeal. He sensed that his colleagues felt angry or threatened when he wanted to look at the virus-typing project from a different viewpoint. But Salk didn't need their support to know his ideas were sound. "They had their fixed procedures and it was my job to comply," he said. "So I did. But there was no reason why I could not also do the work in my own way, and I did."

In his own lab, Salk set a much different tone from the chilly intolerance that bothered him at the professional meetings. Jonas Salk was relaxed and warm with everyone. By 1949, when the virus-typing project officially started, Salk had recruited an outstanding staff that included Dr. Julius Youngner, Byron Bennett, Dr. L. James Lewis, and Salk's secretary Lorraine Friedman.

The team's work began in earnest once the monkeys began arriving. Soon the quarters where the animal cages were kept turned into a popular place. Hospital workers, visitors, even patients, came to see the monkeys. Peter Salk also liked to visit the monkeys when his father brought him to the hospital. Usually the monkeys were quiet. When they became sick, however, they could be dangerous and mean. Sometimes Salk was able to find new homes for his recovered monkeys in zoos. But he couldn't allow himself to grow too fond of them. Many monkeys would have to be sacrificed before a way was found to end polio. Even the viruses Salk used to infect monkeys had originally been grown in other monkeys. Scientists didn't know any other way to get the virus for use in their experiments.

Then in 1949, as Salk was just beginning his project, a

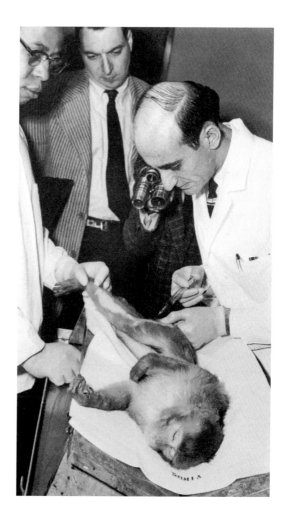

Dr. L. James Lewis, a member of Salk's research team, injects a monkey with poliovirus.

group of researchers led by Dr. John Enders of Children's Hospital in Boston found a way to grow poliovirus outside the body in non-nervous tissue—tissue not from the nerves, spine, or brain of an animal. Enders's team chopped up tissues into tiny pieces and put them into large bottles or test tubes that contained a nourishing fluid. After the cells attached to the sides of the glass and began to thrive, poliovirus was

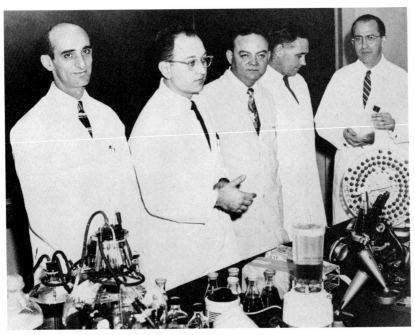

The team of researchers who were typing poliovirus eventually included, left to right, *L. James Lewis, Julius Youngner, Byron Bennett, Percival Bazeley, and Jonas Salk.*

added. The virus then infected the cells and began to multiply. This discovery meant that poliovirus could be produced in the laboratory and would not have to be obtained from the spine or brain of an animal. This exciting breakthrough would save a tremendous amount of time as well as many, many monkeys.

Jonas Salk was intrigued by the possibility of using the new method in his virus-typing project. But when he told the National Foundation he wanted to experiment with Enders's technique, officials would not fund his efforts. He must stick with the original guidelines, they said.

Salk had no choice but to follow the old methods. But he was determined to find out everything he could about what Enders had done. He persuaded the dean of the medical school at the University of Pittsburgh to support him in setting up a tissue-culture lab. And he hired a research assistant, Elsie Ward, to help with the project. Salk told Enders what he wanted to do. He sent Enders unlabeled samples of poliovirus that had already been typed in Salk's Pittsburgh lab. Setting out to retype the samples, Enders introduced each unknown virus into a culture that contained known antibodies. If the virus grew, it was not the type that

Dr. John Enders, winner of the 1954 Nobel Prize in Medicine

the antibodies were directed against. If the virus was destroyed, it was the same type.

In one week, Enders's staff completed their task. Their

Salk explains how monkey kidney tissue is cultivated in test tubes held in roller drums.

results were identical to Salk's results. But working with monkeys, Salk's team had taken several months.

There was no way Salk could ignore such an impressive outcome. Now that he had the equipment and staff he needed, the disapproval of the National Foundation didn't bother him. But once officials learned what he'd already done, the organization gave a belated go-ahead to his tissue-culture work. Supervising every detail of the typing and the culture-growing sometimes kept Salk at the hospital eighteen hours a day. But he thrived on the excitement of being able to type the polioviruses so rapidly.

The fact that Enders's technique allowed the virus to grow in non-nervous tissue was a major milestone. Many people had extreme allergic reactions to any substance obtained from the nervous systems of animals. In 1948 a doctor named Isabel Morgan had published results of her studies on a vaccine made of virus that had been harvested from the nervous systems of monkeys. Although the virus was killed by formaldehyde and the vaccine seemed to work in monkeys, it could not be tried on humans. The risk of a severe, even deadly reaction was too great.

Salk now had a large supply of virus free of any contamination from monkey nervous tissue. Soon he would consider the next critical step—killing the virus grown in the lab and using it to create a vaccine safe for humans.

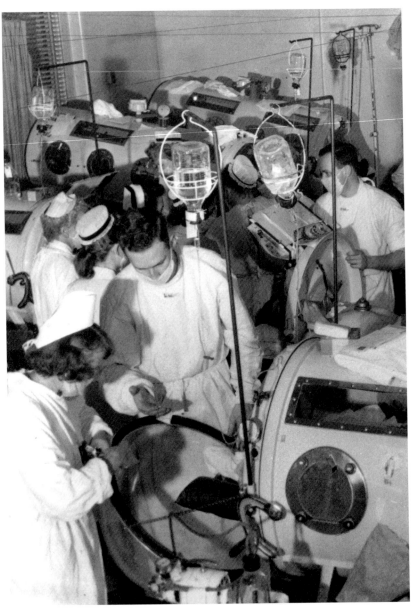

Doctors and nurses swarm around polio patients in iron lungs in a hospital ward in the 1950s.

FIVE

The Best Kept Secret
1950–1952

Although Salk spent most of his time in the lab, sometimes he accompanied other doctors when they made their rounds of polio patients at Municipal Hospital. Every trip through the crowded wards strengthened his desire to end the terrible epidemics. Salk passed bed after bed of frightened children who couldn't move their arms or legs. Other children couldn't even breathe on their own. They were lying in barrel-shaped iron lungs that pushed air into and out of their chests. Only their heads stuck out of the huge, metal machines. Tilting beds helped other children to breathe. The beds swung up and down like seesaws to push the air in and out of the children's lungs. Outwardly, Jonas forced himself to remain calm, but inwardly he suffered with the children.

Throughout the summer polio season, swimming pools, movie theatres, and even playgrounds closed all over the country. People feared they might catch polio in such places. But the epidemics didn't lessen. During this time, Jonas might see as many as sixteen or seventeen ambulances lined up at the emergency room entrance. There weren't enough iron lungs for all the patients who needed them. All hours of the day and night, pleading voices called out to the nurses. Even when the nurses were exhausted, many stayed after their regular shifts to talk to the children and try to make them more comfortable. When they met Jonas Salk in the halls, the nurses and doctors told him "to hurry up and do something." Often they said it in a joking manner, because what they were asking for seemed so impossible.

Salk knew that beneath the rough humor of their demands, they were begging him for a miracle. He also knew that the technology already existed to create such a miracle.

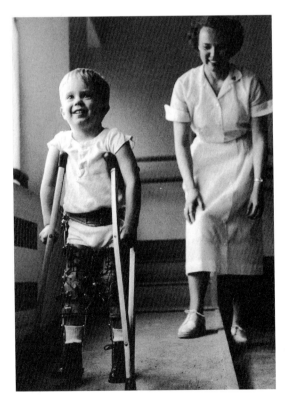

A young boy recovering from polio begins to walk with crutches and leg braces, to the delight of a nurse.

On June 16, 1950, he wrote a letter to Harry Weaver: he was ready "to see if we can develop a satisfactory procedure for the prevention of poliomyelitis by immunologic means."

That same year, Donna and Jonas had another baby boy, and they named him Jonathan. Three little boys made for a lively, noisy home life. But sometimes Jonas stayed so late at work that all he could do was peek in on the boys in bed. Donna took care of the boys on her own and created a supportive environment for Jonas in the evening. A clinical social worker who loved her field, Donna put her professional ambitions on hold to raise her sons and give Jonas the freedom he needed to do his job. When Jonas was at home, he was a patient dad and a good listener. Despite his hectic schedule, Jonas took his family to Oberlin Beach, Ohio, each summer. For several weeks, Jonas could relax and swim with his sons, and just get to know them better. Sometimes he enjoyed simply lying in a hammock or playing word games. But he also brought scientific papers to work on. And he wanted to know what was going on in the lab. Since the only telephone in the summer colony hung from a utility pole across from the children's play area several cottages away, it wasn't always easy to carry on conversations with colleagues—especially in rainy weather. Finally, the Salks became the first family to put a telephone in their rented cottage so Jonas could stay in touch with the research team more easily.

As much as he enjoyed vacations, Jonas was always ready to return to his lab. Even at home in the evenings, he couldn't take his mind off his work. What did the data mean? Was there a new approach he could try? Once Donna complained that he hadn't heard a word she was saying. "My dear, I'm giving you my undevoted attention," replied Jonas absently. Then realizing what he'd said, he had to admit that Donna had a point.

What really got Salk's undivided attention during this time were the viruses growing in his lab. Like the influenza virus, each type of poliovirus had many slight variations called strains. Unlike influenza, however, one strain of poliovirus conferred immunity against all other strains of the same type. Salk had had to include as many strains as possible in his flu vaccine to give people the greatest immunity. But he would only need to include one strain from each type of poliovirus in his polio vaccine. That way, one shot would protect against all strains of the three types of polio. The only question was which strains to use.

Salk's team grew many different strains in the tissue cultures they had established in test tubes and large flasks. After harvesting each strain, they added virus fluid to test tubes of thriving monkey cells. The medium in which these monkey cells grew contained phenol red dye to monitor their health. The tubes were placed in a rotating device so that the virus fluid could rhythmically lap all the cells. This would nourish all the cells and give the virus the best chance to attack them. If many cells remained alive, the dye turned yellowish. This indicated that the virus was not growing. If the virus grew and killed most of the cells, however, the color in the test tube remained red.

Salk and his team tested many strains to see which grew most easily and which were best at inducing antibodies. Three strains turned out to be the best suited for the vaccine. To Salk's surprise, they were among the first strains he had tested. Even after years of searching, he never found any better strains. "A fantastic accident," he labeled the coincidence.

With the help of his staff, Salk grew vast amounts of these viruses. The next step was to "cook" them with a chemical

Salk looks on as Dr. Mary Lynch Bailey prepares tubes for cultures of poliovirus.

called formaldehyde. Cooking was the term he used for inactivating or killing the virus, even though no heat was involved in the process. In fact, he once compared making a vaccine to creating a new kind of cake. The cook "starts with an idea and certain ingredients and then experiments, a little more of this and a little less of that, and keeps changing things until finally she has a good recipe."

Part of a recipe is knowing how long something has to cook. Salk had to know how long to "cook" the poliovirus in the formaldehyde. He couldn't risk even one virus particle surviving the process. The one live virus might cause the polio it was supposed to prevent. But if Salk cooked the virus too long, the killed virus particles might lose the ability to trigger the production of antibodies.

Even after the success of the flu vaccine during World War II, many scientists were convinced that a killed-virus vaccine wouldn't work against polio. Albert Sabin was an especially vocal opponent. He argued that the immunity wouldn't last. The antibodies created in response to the killed virus would disappear after a while. A person could become susceptible to polio again without even knowing it. Sabin believed that one of the virus strains he and others were developing for use as a live-virus vaccine would get better results because the immunity would last longer. They hoped to weaken the virus so it wouldn't cause polio but would still reproduce in the body.

Many other scientists respected Jonas Salk's approach. In 1951 the National Foundation chose him to attend the Second International Poliomyelitis Congress to be held in Copenhagen, Denmark. Jonas sailed to Europe on the same ship as John Enders, Albert Sabin, and other noted researchers. But Jonas preferred to spend much of his time alone on deck, watching the waves and thinking about his research. He had come a long way. The ocean trip was a chance to relax and to quietly take stock of his situation—something his hectic routine rarely allowed. Sailing home after an exhilarating conference, Jonas became well acquainted with a fellow passenger. Although he had previously met Basil O'Connor, the lawyer who headed the National Foundation for Infantile Paralysis, Jonas didn't really know him well.

O'Connor was getting a little tired of meetings. There was a sharp edge to several of his remarks, and he aimed some of his discontent at Salk. The other scientists at the dinner table were amazed by Salk's lively comebacks. O'Connor was intrigued. More than that, he was moved by the sensitive way

Salk treated O'Connor's adult daughter, Bettyann Culver, who was recovering from polio. When Salk learned how worried and upset the young woman still was, he sought her out. Tactfully, he helped her sort through her fears and develop a positive view of her future. A grateful Basil O'Connor decided he wanted to know more about the soft-spoken and kind, yet proud and tough scientist. As they walked around the deck or talked together in the swimming pool, O'Connor realized that Salk was brilliant and dedicated and shared his vision of helping others. The two became close friends.

Basil O'Connor, president of the National Foundation for Infantile Paralysis, stands on the deck of the Queen Mary.

When Salk arrived back in Pittsburgh, he resumed his frantic pace in the lab. The research team, which now included Dr. Percival L. Bazeley and Dr. Ulrich Krech, faced numerous challenges. Youngner and Ward tested different types of monkey tissue to see which fostered the fastest growth of poliovirus. They also discovered new ways to measure how much virus they had grown and how much antibody was produced in the blood. Working on experimental vaccines, Bennett explored the best way to kill the virus with formaldehyde. Lewis studied the safety of the killed viruses in monkeys.

Carefully, Salk developed guidelines to ensure that every last bit of the virus was killed. He also supervised experiments in which chemical substances called adjuvants were added to the killed virus particles in order to boost antibody production.

Relying on both intuition and logic, Salk sometimes wondered what it would be like to be a virus. How would a virus protect itself? Then he turned the problem around and imagined himself as the immune system. What would he do to defeat the army of invading viruses? No one in medical school had taught him to think this way, but he found his creative musings helpful. On the more mechanical side, he developed several innovative techniques and devices that are still used in tissue-culture labs.

As the polio season of 1952 approached, Salk continued to devote his time and energy to conquering the disease. Nothing could be done to prevent thousands of cases of polio that year, but the sooner he perfected a vaccine, the sooner children would be safe. Salk had already tested several vaccine preparations on monkeys. None of the monkeys got sick, and all of them developed antibodies in their blood. It was time to test the vaccine on humans.

Fifteen miles away in the suburb of Leetsdale was a health facility called the D. T. Watson Home for Crippled Children. Many young polio victims lived there as they went through therapy to build up their muscles. Salk visited the home in May 1952 and talked with the administrators about what he wanted to do. He explained that the children would be safe, because before he inoculated them, he would test their blood to see what type of antibodies they had. Then he would use a vaccine with only that type of killed virus. Because the children already had antibodies, they couldn't get polio again. Afterward, Salk would take another blood sample to see if the vaccine had boosted their antibody levels even higher. That would tell Salk if the vaccine was doing what it was supposed to do.

The administrators of the Watson Home were very impressed with Salk. He explained things well, and he took a great interest in the children at the home. He cared deeply about their feelings and their needs as well as about the results of his experiments. And he believed so strongly in his vaccine that nurses and patients couldn't help but believe in it too. Both parents and administrators agreed that the polio vaccine should be tested at the D. T. Watson Home.

But Salk had one more request. He needed his experiments to be kept a secret. It was too soon to let the public know what he was doing, he explained. If word leaked out, reporters would be clamoring to know more. Salk would have his hands full enough evaluating the vaccine. There would be no time to deal with news crews. Besides, no vaccine would be available for general use for a long time, certainly not for the approaching polio season.

All the children, parents, and nurses at the Watson Home agreed to keep the secret. The next month, Salk returned to

Children recovering from polio work on their leg exercises. Their bodies have developed antibodies to the type of polio they contracted.

the home to get the blood samples he needed. On July 2, he began giving the shots. By this time, the children were already beginning to think of him as a friend. Getting a shot was no fun, but talking to Dr. Salk was. He was funny and sympathetic and ready to listen to anything. Chatting with Dr. Salk almost made you forget the needle he slipped quickly into your arm. He never let you forget how important you were or that he was very grateful that you were part of his test.

The night after the first shots, a restless Jonas couldn't sleep. He had to drive back to the Watson Home just to see for himself that everyone was fine. The nurses assured him that no one was sick, and Jonas knew, from his careful tests, that the vaccine was safe. But Jonas continued to think of the children constantly—and visit often. The cook became so fond of him that she made his favorite strawberry pie for each visit. The children were delighted that Dr. Salk remembered all their names and could pick up week-old conversations exactly where they'd left off.

Salk knew that the more he tested his preparations, the sooner he could make a vaccine available to the public. The next step was to inoculate people who had not had polio. After consulting with the Watson Home staff, he injected some volunteers from the staff and members of the patients' families with a vaccine against all three types of polio. It took a great deal of faith to proceed to this critical stage. If word of his actions had leaked out, it would have been sensational news. "I couldn't [have done] it unless I was more critical of myself than others were of me," Salk said.

More subjects were needed to test the vaccine. Salk especially wanted to test "triple negatives," people without antibodies to any of the three poliovirus types. Salk had also made arrangements to test his preparation at the Polk School, a facility for mentally handicapped men and boys. These men and boys had not had polio either. Officials at the Polk School agreed to the tests because they felt it was in their patients' best interest to be immunized against polio. The patients didn't understand the significance of what Jonas was doing, but they responded to his gentleness and warmth. And they liked the lollipops he gave them.

Jonas continued to call and to visit both institutions. No one became ill from this round of immunizations. The polio vaccine was safe. But was it also effective? Had it stimulated the production of antibodies that could protect children and adults against polio? That was the burning question that Salk had to answer.

Salk at his microscope in the Municipal Hospital lab

$\text{⑤}\text{①}\text{⊗}$

In the Spotlight

1952–1953

$\mathbf{B}$ack in his lab, Salk studied blood samples from the children he'd immunized in July. He started by adding poliovirus to tissue cultures growing in test tubes. Unchecked, the virus would kill all the tissue's cells. He then added blood samples to each tube. If the blood samples contained antibodies, the virus would be destroyed and the cells would remain healthy.

Tense with the drama of the moment, Jonas placed tube after tube under the microscope. With mounting excitement, he realized that he finally had scientific proof of what he had known all along. The level of antibody in the polio patients' blood had risen dramatically since their vaccination. The vaccine worked. Seeing the proof under the microscope was the biggest thrill of his entire life. Elated, Jonas shared his findings first with Donna. "I've got it," he exclaimed.

Donna was delighted but not surprised. She had anticipated this moment all along. "I mean, Jonas, when you put your mind to something . . . " she began. There wasn't any need to finish the sentence.

Then Jonas told the staff of the Watson Home. They had believed in Dr. Salk all along, too. They were as thrilled as he was to think that his work would keep other children from suffering as their patients did.

Several months later, in December 1952, Salk took new blood samples from the children and adults who had been vaccinated at the Watson Home and the Polk School. To his satisfaction, their antibody levels remained at the same high levels as the September measurements. This meant their immunity was as strong as ever. Salk had proved that the vaccine was safe, effective, and lasting—at least long enough for one polio season. It was time to share his findings with other polio researchers.

In January 1953, the National Foundation's Committee of Immunization met in Hershey, Pennsylvania. On his way to the meeting, Albert Sabin stopped by to visit Jonas at his lab. Courteously, Jonas discussed polio research with his rival and invited him to his house for dinner. The two men traveled by train together to Hershey. But Jonas saved his big news for the meeting. Matter-of-factly, he explained that he had safely immunized people and obtained highly promising results.

The committee members were stunned by the announcement. Almost at once, the meeting was plunged into intense debate. A few members were so enthusiastic that they wanted a nationwide field test of the vaccine. In 1952, the previous summer, the polio epidemic had been the worst on record. More children had died from polio than from any other infectious disease. Whatever could be done to save lives and prevent paralysis needed to be done as soon as possible, these members reasoned.

Sabin and Salk talk with each other at a meeting of polio researchers.

Other researchers said that Jonas Salk was not nearly ready to test his preparation safely. There were still too many unknowns, too many experiments to try. It would take years to figure out the best way to immunize the general population. Albert Sabin was one of the loudest voices urging Jonas to go slowly and cautiously.

Caught between these two arguments, Salk wanted to hop right back on the train to Pittsburgh. Instead, he stayed an extra day in Hershey to help Harry Weaver write a speech about Salk's success for the foundation's board of trustees. Salk still wanted the details of trial immunizations kept as secret as possible. Too much publicity would interfere with his work and create too much excitement too soon.

But even a toned-down version of Salk's accomplishment was bound to raise hopes. The day after Weaver's speech, Jonas's carefully kept secret was out. The new polio vaccine made headlines all over the world. Salk was caught in a dilemma. On the one hand, the National Foundation welcomed the publicity, hoping it would encourage people to give money to the March of Dimes. On the other, scientists were supposed to present their work to other scientists before going public with it. This gave their colleagues a chance to study the findings and offer criticism and suggestions. The support of other experts lent credibility to the research. The early publicity Salk received irritated some other scientists.

Salk's predicament got even worse when the national gossip columnist Earl Wilson published a story on the polio vaccine a few days before Salk's scientific paper was due to appear in the *Journal of the American Medical Association*. "New Polio Vaccine—Big Hopes Seen," claimed Wilson.

As far as Salk was concerned, Wilson's story was the last straw. Furious, he dropped everything in the lab and rushed to New York to see Basil O'Connor. Salk knew he couldn't stop the publicity, but maybe he could control it. He told O'Connor he wanted to go on national radio to tell everyone what was really happening. He couldn't bear for parents to get their hopes up for protective measures that weren't ready yet. O'Connor agreed.

Two days before his paper appeared in the medical journal, Jonas Salk discussed his research on the radio. No scientist had ever done this before. But no other scientist had ever faced a public so eager—even desperate—for knowledge. "Although progress has been more rapid than we had any right to expect, there will be no vaccine available for widespread use the next polio season," Salk said.

As soon as his speech was over, Salk packed up his notes, grabbed his coat, and left for the train station. He traveled all night and went straight to his lab the next morning without even stopping at home. He would much rather *do* his work than talk about it.

That spring, Salk asked Dr. Robert Nix, the pediatrician at the Watson Home, to help him find volunteers from the nearby area to receive the vaccine. He was still experimenting to see which preparations worked best and what levels of antibodies he could produce in the blood. After Dr. Nix found numerous volunteers, Salk scheduled the shots for Saturday mornings at the Watson Home.

Sometimes Jonas's sons came with him, wandering over the lush, green lawns of the Watson Home while their father was busy. They had already received their own shots at home. Assembling the family around the kitchen table one day in the fall of 1952, Jonas inoculated Donna and the boys against polio. At two years old, Jonathan was the youngest person ever to receive the polio vaccine.

Later, Jonas called his cousin Helen in New York and announced, "I'm ready." Immediately she brought her three children to Jonas for shots. Helen's friends thought she was acting impulsively, but Helen had trusted Jonas from childhood. "If he says so, it's okay with me," she declared.

Every weekend Salk vaccinated or took blood samples from hundreds of children. His experiments generated a great deal of publicity and excitement. Soon, in fact, people were calling asking to be part of the new trial. They believed the vaccine would protect their children and grandchildren from polio. Many friends of Jonas and Donna, including Harry

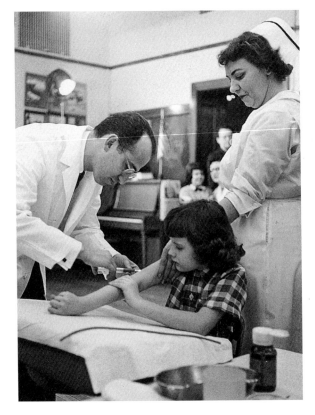

*Salk vaccinates
a child in 1953.*

Weaver, brought their children for polio shots. As momentum
grew, Helen got calls from the same friends who had tried to
caution her earlier. They wanted polio shots too. Jonas sent a
batch of vaccine to a New York doctor to inoculate his cousin's
friends.

At the Municipal Hospital and at the Watson Home, Salk
kept track of dozens of details. Nothing happened without his
knowledge. But things were happening at the National Foundation that he knew nothing about. One day he read in the
newspaper that national testing of his vaccine was scheduled
to begin in the fall of 1953.

That was only months away. Small scale testing was one thing, but providing vast quantities of vaccine all over the country was another. His own lab certainly couldn't produce enough. Where would all the vaccine come from? Who would make certain it was safe?

Salk was shocked. And he was angry. No one had the right to make such a decision without consulting him. Once more, Salk took the train to New York to see Basil O'Connor. As much as he admired and respected O'Connor, he wasn't even sure that they could remain friends.

Salk began their meeting by carefully explaining all the issues he was still working on. How much formaldehyde should be used to kill the virus? At what temperature should it be killed? Could mineral oil be successfully used as an adjuvant to boost antibody production? There were other questions as well. How many shots should be given? How much time should elapse between shots for maximum production of antibodies?

Basil O'Connor listened carefully. "Now I don't want you to worry about a thing, Jonas," he said. "It's your work and nothing will be done with it that you don't want. . . . Just tell me one thing: Do you think it's possible—all I mean is possible—that you might come up with something for a field trial by the end of this year or the beginning of the next?"

Jonas's fears evaporated. He wasn't being asked to *promise* anything. "Yes, it's *possible,*" he replied. Nothing more needed to be said.

Scientists work in the laboratories of a commercial drug company to make the polio vaccine.

SEVEN

Planning a Miracle
1953–1954

No one was more anxious than Jonas Salk himself for the widespread use of a polio vaccine. That summer, four hundred patients were admitted to Pittsburgh's Municipal Hospital with polio. The thought of these suffering children was never far from Salk's mind, but he had little time to visit the wards.

Things were moving rapidly. Late in 1953, Thomas Francis was asked to evaluate results, should there be a field test. Many scientists felt it should be a double-blind study. That meant that some of the children injected would get the vaccine and some would get a harmless substance called a placebo. But Salk felt badly about giving some children a substance that wouldn't do them any good. Some of them would become ill during the summer polio season. The number of children who received a placebo and got polio would then be compared to the number of vaccinated children who got polio. Although this would help prove the effectiveness of the vaccine, Salk felt terrible. The welfare of all children was his prime

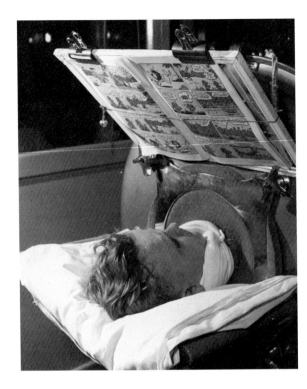

This polio patient needs an iron lung to breathe. He also needs a nurse to turn the pages of his comic book.

concern. He hated for any youngsters to suffer when he had a vaccine that would protect them.

Francis insisted on the double-blind test and the use of a placebo. Although Salk still wanted to immunize as many children as possible, he knew the field test had to convince other scientists. Salk respected Francis and knew he would do an excellent job of analyzing the data from the field test. Yes, he told his old professor, he would agree to the double-blind test.

No one had actually decided yet if there would be a field test. But everyone, including Salk, was acting as if there would be. The National Foundation wanted to test the vaccine in the spring of 1954 on hundreds of thousands of children from all over the United States. Their plans called for using "observed controls" in addition to the placebo-controlled portion of the trial. In the observed control areas, all participating second graders would receive vaccine. The polio rate for these children would be compared to unvaccinated first and third graders in the same areas.

By this time, Jonas was arriving at work long before class began each day for his sons. Donna took the boys to school, even though it meant a long drive into the city twice a day. When school was over, the boys knew they could count on their mom's car to be first in line to pick them up. With Donna in charge of the family, Jonas didn't have to worry about a thing outside his work. He could focus all his energy on defeating polio.

Soon Jonas was so busy he didn't even have time to drive the half hour to and from work. Finally in November of 1953, the Salks left their country home and moved into the city so Jonas could be closer to his lab. Even so, Jonas often left home before dawn and returned around midnight. In the mornings, he handed out slips of paper to each member of his staff with instructions for the day's work. Busy dealing with the details of arrangements for a possible field trial, Jonas often didn't get back to the research team until the next day. When Jonas was exhausted, he'd close his eyes for a brief catnap at his desk. Often he worked straight through meals, hurriedly eating a sandwich at his desk.

If his family and staff members saw less of Salk these days, the American public saw more. Men and women were fascinated by the glimpses newspapers provided of the likeable and dedicated scientist who believed he could save their children from polio. Salk, however, was distressed by the publicity—especially when reporters asked questions about his personal life. "Why do they all want to know what I had for breakfast?" he complained to John Troan, one of the few reporters with whom he felt comfortable.

But reporters wanted more than the details of his home life. They wanted to photograph his lab and describe what went on there. By the time they came in, set up cameras, and talked to technicians in different parts of the lab, a whole day would be gone. Jonas found the situation infuriating. One time a photographer, wanting a dramatic picture, asked him to hold a rack of test tubes so high that it slipped from Jonas's grasp and crashed to the floor. The news crew, sure that polio germs were spreading all across the floor, fled the lab in panic. Jonas was left all alone to clean the area with formaldehyde.

Besides the inconvenience of their presence, Jonas was unhappy with reporters' use of the words "Salk vaccine." "It's not the Salk vaccine," he stressed over and over again to Basil O'Connor. "It embarrasses me with my colleagues to have it called 'Salk vaccine.' I'm not entitled to that kind of credit and everyone knows it."

By "everyone," Jonas meant other doctors and scientists whose contributions to polio research had enabled him to make a vaccine in the first place. He didn't want anyone to think he was trying to grab all the credit or promote himself. Hoping to appease Jonas, O'Connor told his own staff not to use the term "Salk vaccine." But there was nothing he could do about the general public, and he told Jonas not to waste time worrying what the vaccine was called. "The whole world was waiting for [the vaccine] and everyone wanted to know who developed it," O'Connor recalled. "The scientist turned out to be a nice fellow named Salk, whose name fit conveniently into headlines. The vaccine was going to be called the Salk vaccine whether he liked it or not."

Salk, at work in his lab, holds up a rack of test tubes for a news photographer.

An enormous supply of vaccine was needed for the field test—much more than Salk's lab could supply. Salk and the National Foundation turned to commercial drug companies for help. Anxious to preserve the safety and strength of the vaccine, Jonas carefully adjusted his guidelines for mass production. Then he began using these same guidelines on a smaller scale in his lab. He wanted to test for himself the exact procedure that would be used to produce the vaccine for the field trial.

Soon problems began to surface. One team of researchers claimed they had been unable to kill poliovirus by following Salk's instructions. Challenged by Salk, one of the researchers agreed that they might not have used a long enough exposure to formaldehyde in tissue cultures that had an especially high concentration of virus. Despite his concession, doubt lingered in the minds of many doctors. As if this wasn't bad enough, Albert Sabin continued to question Salk's work and the safety of a large-scale field test. Salk believed so firmly in his vaccine that he said, "There is no question of 'how safe' it is. It is safe and it can't be safer than safe."

In preparation for a possible field test, the National Institutes of Health (NIH) was testing batches of commercially produced vaccine. On March 22, Salk returned to his office after giving shots at a local school. Opening his mail, he found an alarming report from the NIH. Commercial vaccine had given polio to monkeys. The field test might have to be put off at least a year. Anxiously, Jonas dropped his work and hurried to Maryland to find out what had happened.

Investigations revealed that two of the drug companies had made serious errors. One forgot to filter the virus fluid before killing it. Another did not expose the virus to formaldehyde long enough. As a result, live poliovirus was found in some of the vaccine these companies made. Although two batches of the vaccine were rejected, NIH officials decided that a national field test was still feasible.

In spite of the confidence of the NIH, the controversy

about the vaccine's safety dragged on. Albert Sabin continued to oppose the field test vehemently. Rumors about the defective commercial vaccine got blown out of proportion. On April 4, Walter Winchell, a popular radio broadcaster, opened his program on a note of panic. "Attention everyone!" he declared. "In a few minutes I will report on a new polio vaccine—it may be a killer!" Winchell went on to declare that live virus had been found in seven out of ten batches of the vaccine. Immediately the National Foundation issued a denial. But the mistaken report, which Winchell had received from a popular writer, caused a great deal of confusion and alarm among medical professionals as well as parents.

Would there be a field test or not? Walter Winchell's report made the National Foundation's job even more difficult. Everything was set. Vaccine had been made, tested, and shipped. Doctors and nurses in forty-four states were ready to begin inoculations. But the National Foundation's specially appointed Vaccine Advisory Committee still hadn't given the go-ahead for the gigantic experiment. Time was running out if the field test was to take place before the summer polio season of 1954. On April 23, 1954, the committee, representatives from the drug companies, and officials from the NIH met in Bethesda, Maryland, to make their decision.

Outside the meeting room, Jonas waited nervously. "Why aren't you in there?" someone asked him.

"They are voting now," said Jonas. "It's not my decision to make." After months of ceaseless activity, there was nothing Jonas Salk could do but wait.

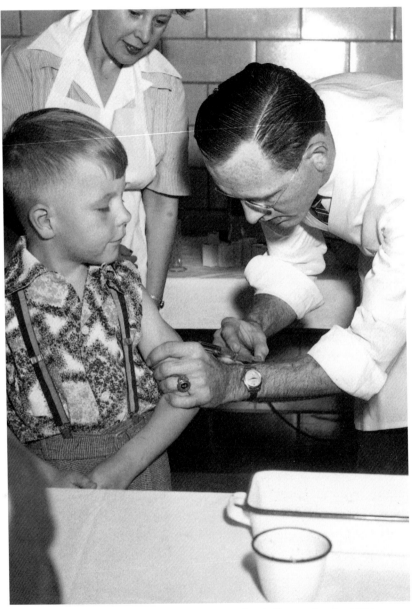

*Six-year-old Randy Kerr gets a shot of the Salk vaccine in 1954
and becomes the first Polio Pioneer.*

⒠ⓘⒼⒽⓉ

Triumph and Tragedy

1954–1955

Jonas's waiting was over. The committee voted that the field test should go forward. On April 26, 1954, a six-year-old boy named Randy Kerr became the first youngster to receive the vaccine in the nationwide field test. The biggest experiment in medical history had begun.

That night, Basil O'Connor and Jonas Salk made a second radio presentation. "I do not share the view of those who feel that polio has been with us a long time, and therefore we can live with it another year," Salk declared. The time had come to conquer polio.

Over the next few weeks, the country followed the story avidly. A Gallup Poll revealed that more Americans knew about the field trial than knew the full name of the president! More than one million first, second, and third graders all over the country took part in the field test. Over 600,000 of these children, called Polio Pioneers, received a series of three injections. No one—not even Jonas—knew who received the vaccine and who got the placebo.

Salk continued to attend conferences and to test batches of vaccine made by the drug companies. To his dismay, he found that some of the vaccine was weaker than expected. Over Salk's objections, the NIH had made the companies add a substance that was not in his original preparations. Even though there hadn't been time to test Merthiolate, NIH officials felt it would make the vaccine safer by killing any bacteria found in the vaccine. But as Salk had feared, Merthiolate turned out to lessen the vaccine's ability to induce polio antibodies. Salk was deeply concerned that many of the Polio Pioneers would not get the same degree of protection as the children he'd vaccinated in Pittsburgh.

This was a difficult and stressful time for Jonas. He knew some scientists believed he had rushed into the field test too soon. Only the results could prove they were wrong. But it took Dr. Francis and his staff nearly one year to sift through all the data, comparing the polio rates of the vaccinated children with the unvaccinated. As he discovered more weak batches of vaccine, Jonas had to wonder what the results would be.

Finally in April 1955, Thomas Francis was ready to make his report public. Did the vaccine really protect against polio? Parents all over the world breathlessly awaited the verdict. Although Jonas had always gone on professional trips alone, he took his wife and three sons with him to Ann Arbor where Dr. Francis would be speaking. At ages eleven, eight, and four, Peter, Darrell, and Jonathan were old enough to understand the importance, if not the details, of their father's work. Whatever Dr. Francis said, Jonas wanted them to hear it with him.

On April 12, the morning of the announcement, Dr. Francis approached Jonas at breakfast. A hush fell over the table as Jonas and his companions waited for Francis to speak. The moment of truth was at hand. Yes, Francis told a greatly relieved Jonas. The

Jonas talks to, left to right, *Darrell, Donna, Jonathan, and Peter.*

vaccine worked. Grinning, Jonas shook hands with his former teacher and several other scientists in the faculty dining room.

Hours later, Jonas Salk was seated on the stage of the University of Michigan's Rackham Hall while Dr. Francis announced the results of his study. Five hundred doctors and scientists as well as Salk's family and members of his research team listened to Francis's speech from the vast auditorium. Francis's detailed studies proved that the vaccine was sixty to seventy percent effective in preventing type I polio and ninety percent or more effective in preventing types II and III.

From left: *Salk, Francis, and O'Connor are surrounded by cameras, microphones, and reporters at a press conference on April 12, 1955.*

When Salk took the podium, the audience clapped loudly. Deeply moved, Salk stressed that the polio vaccine was the result of a team effort in his lab. No one person was responsible. He also said that the work he'd done since the field test began could lead to a vaccine that was one hundred percent effective.

Millions of people heard the news on radio and television. Parents everywhere hailed Jonas Salk's triumph. Church bells rang. Sirens blared. Loudspeakers broadcast the news into busy department stores. That very afternoon, Oveta Culp Hobby, secretary of the U.S. Department of Health, Education, and Welfare, licensed the vaccine for immediate use. Now all children could have access to polio shots. "It's a great day," Hobby declared. "It's a wonderful day for the whole world. It's a history-making day."

Yet in some ways it was a very difficult day for Jonas Salk. "Unreal" is how he described it. Throughout the afternoon, Salk sensed that some of his colleagues were annoyed and angered by his speech. Even Dr. Francis told Salk it was much too soon to speak about a vaccine that was one hundred percent effective. Jonas knew that parents desperately wanted the latest information on his research. The reaction of his colleagues disappointed him. Ever cautious about protocol, they thought he had said too much.

As reporters milled around and cameras flashed, the day seemed to turn into a circus. Many scientists felt the occasion called for a more serious atmosphere. In this regard, Jonas agreed with them. All he wanted to do was return to his lab as quickly as possible. In the midst of the commotion, one colleague, Dr. Alan Gregg, managed to ask about Jonas's future after his work on polio was completed.

"I'm not sure what I'll want to do," replied Jonas.

"Jonas, do only that which makes your heart leap," counseled Gregg. It was electrifying advice, but Jonas had no time to think about it yet. That night, he appeared on Edward R. Murrow's television program *See It Now*. Salk had met the noted broadcaster earlier that year. He admired Murrow for his serious and intelligent approach to issues. Here was someone he could enjoy talking with. Murrow didn't ask Jonas questions about his hobbies or favorite foods. Tonight Murrow asked who owned the patent to the new vaccine.

"Well, the people, I would say," Salk replied with a broad smile. "There is no patent. Could you patent the sun?" Salk believed that everyone had an equal right to good health. A patent would simply confuse the issue.

Edward R. Murrow, left, *talks with Salk during a break in filming his television program* See It Now.

After the broadcast, Murrow took Jonas aside for a private word. He said a terrible tragedy had just befallen his friend: Jonas Salk had lost his anonymity. He meant that

Donna watches while Jonas plays with the boys during their 1955 stay in Ann Arbor.

Jonas's previous publicity was nothing compared to the scrutiny he'd soon receive as a major celebrity.

Murrow's words proved prophetic. The Salks had only planned to stay in Ann Arbor for a night or two, but letters, telegrams, phone calls, and offers poured in from all over the country. The family was forced to stay a week just so Jonas could cope with the avalanche. Tom Coleman, the press agent who answered the phone for Jonas, spent so much time talking that he lost his voice. At dinner that night, everyone found themselves politely copying his husky whispers. Peter, Darrell, and Jonathan were eager to get home and tired of wearing suits. Quietly, Donna oversaw their activities in what she called "the eye of the hurricane."

Messages continued to arrive in staggering numbers. A Hollywood studio wanted to make a movie of Jonas's life. A hospital on the West Coast wanted to change its name to the Jonas E. Salk Memorial Hospital. "Memorials are for dead people," Jonas replied with characteristic humor. "I'm only half dead at this time." He declined the honor.

When the Salks finally returned to Pittsburgh, they found the mayor's car waiting to take them home. Even in his lab, Jonas couldn't escape reporters. He was forced to hold a press conference his first day back at work. "I have a laboratory furnished by funds," he told reporters. "Do I use it or do I become a movie star?"

Still the media dogged him. On another occasion, a reporter asked Jonas if he were trying to find a vaccine for the common cold. "All I'm trying to do is keep my balance," Jonas quipped. Mail continued to arrive by the truckload. The town of Amarillo, Texas, sent Jonas a new car. He sold it and returned the money to Amarillo to pay for polio shots.

The Salk family was still adjusting to its sudden fame

just days after their return when a summons came from Washington. Jonas Salk was to receive a special citation from President Eisenhower. Soon the Salks were on their way to the airport, running late and snarled in heavy traffic. Finally they stopped at a police station and asked for help. Several motorcycle officers roared ahead of the Salk car, stopping traffic so the family could make it to the airport on time. As the plane approached Washington, Salk composed a short speech to remind the nation that many people had contributed to the success of the vaccine. After he received

Jonas Salk receives an award from President Eisenhower in 1955.

the award, Salk stood on the front steps of the White House and declared, "On behalf of all the people, in laboratories, in the field and those behind the lines, I gladly accept this recognition of what each of us has contributed."

When the Salks returned home, Jonas hoped that he could finally resume his normal lab routine. Then a few days later came devastating news. Several children had gotten polio after receiving the vaccine. For an instant, his entire world collapsed. But Jonas knew he could not give in to panic. Steeling himself to remain calm, he gathered what facts he could about the new cases of polio. He spent the next day in his office, answering the emergency string of telephones that had been set up. Terrified doctors wanted to know what they could do for patients and for their own children who had received the vaccine. Jonas counseled each caller not to panic and to give the vaccinated children a substance called gamma globulin. Tested in 1951, this blood product contained antibodies to the disease. Although these antibodies would disappear in a month or six weeks, gamma globulin often provided short-term immunity to polio. That might be enough time to stem panic and preserve health during the crisis. But nothing could help the children who were already paralyzed.

Throughout his whole career, Jonas had longed to make a positive difference in people's lives. The thought that his vaccine might have given children polio was unbearable. Only one thing got him through that terrible day. He knew that rightly made, the vaccine was absolutely safe. He was determined to find out what had gone wrong.

The next day, Salk arrived in Bethesda, Maryland, for meetings with other scientists and officials of the U.S. Public Health Service. Every day new polio cases were reported in children who'd recently been vaccinated. Heartsick, Salk felt

During a March of Dimes fundraiser in the mid-1950s, Richard McPherson, left, and his mother, Marie, center, help hold a poster that voices everyone's determination to put an end to polio.

as if he knew the young victims and their parents. Each new case was a fresh sorrow to him.

Salk was upset with the NIH for not monitoring the production process more carefully. After the vaccine had been licensed, the government had stopped inspecting each batch for safety. Instead, it simply relied on the manufacturers' inspections. One of the drug companies had not followed Salk's precise instructions. Fluid with virus had been stored so long that a layer of sediment had formed around the particles. This layer protected the virus when it was treated with formaldehyde. Still-living virus found its way into the vaccine.

Salk was furious. He was sure that no problems would have occurred if the manufacturers had stuck to the same rigid standards he had used making the vaccine in his own lab.

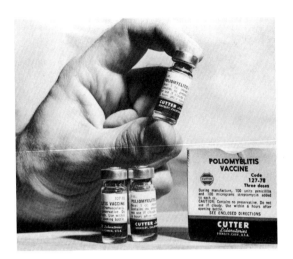

*Vials of the Salk
vaccine made by
Cutter Laboratories
were withdrawn
following the
outbreak of polio in
vaccinated children.*

Many people at the meetings didn't see it that way. Albert
Sabin questioned the vaccine's safety under any standards.
Sometimes Salk felt as if his critics hated him. He always
spoke quietly, but inside he was seething. After the day's
meetings, he returned to his hotel room and wrote angry
speeches to deliver the next day. Then, more relaxed, he
would throw the speeches away and go to bed. Salk knew he
had to keep a tight rein on his feelings. The future of the
whole vaccination program depended on him.

Within days, however, the program was suspended, and
Salk was greatly upset. Over five million children had safely
received polio shots. Now many others would be forced to go
without protection.

Intense examinations revealed that only one company,
Cutter Laboratories, had made vaccine in which living virus
had been found. New rules were drawn up to test each batch
of vaccine. "The margin of safety is now so clearly understood
that only the grossest human error can upset it," Salk
declared. By the end of May, children were lining up for

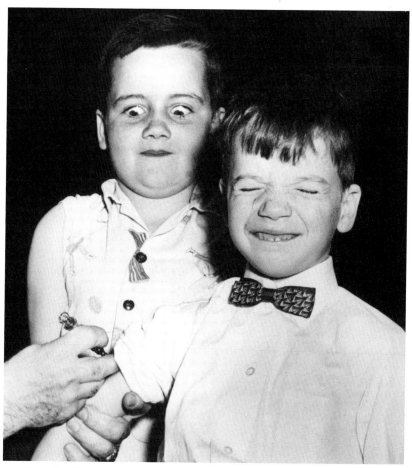

After the Salk vaccine was proven safe, children all over the country had to face shots.

polio shots again. Eventually 204 cases of polio were traced to live virus present in the vaccine incorrectly made by Cutter Laboratories. After this tragic episode, no one got polio from the vaccine.

Salk and O'Connor speak about the killed-virus vaccine at a news conference in 1955. A question from a reporter brings a smile to Salk's face.

ⓃⒾⓃⒺ

The Perfect Setting

1955–1960

Jonas Salk wanted nothing more than to pursue his research uninterrupted. Scarcely a day went by when he didn't talk about getting back to the lab. But invitations poured in from all over the country. Scientific organizations wanted him to come and speak. Other groups simply wanted to give him awards. Tactfully, Jonas declined events planned to honor him. He did, however, speak about the vaccine and his theories of immunology at many meetings.

Perhaps more than anything else, Jonas needed time to think. His mind was constantly churning with ideas, both scientific and philosophic. Jonas wanted to share these creative concepts with laypeople as well as other scientists. Needing a quiet retreat, he lugged a folding table, chair, and some shelves up to his unused third floor. Jonas liked writing at the top of his house, surrounded by books and papers. In fact, he wrote so much and collected so many awards, articles, and manuscripts that papers and objects spilled over every surface.

In spite of incessant demands on his time, Jonas still

managed to take several weeks each summer to be with his family. Beginning in 1957, the Salks spent their summer vacation at Deep Creek, Maryland, where Jonas enjoyed barbecuing, swimming, and sailing with his sons. They also went waterskiing as the boys got older. Balanced precariously on a single ski, the boys sometimes teased their dad because he preferred the comparative safety of two skis.

Over the next few years, Salk was happy to see the polio rate drop drastically. But the disease didn't disappear entirely. Salk knew it could if all children were vaccinated. He wanted large-scale programs where children could be inoculated free or for a very small sum. He vehemently opposed the approach of the American Medical Association (AMA) that the vaccine should only be given in doctors' offices. He read about one doctor who made three thousand dollars in one afternoon just by giving polio shots. "What are you going to do with people like that?" he cried angrily. "Six hundred kids who have five dollars get vaccinated, and six hundred who do not have five dollars do not get vaccinated."

Salk spoke out publicly, urging everyone fifty years old or younger to get inoculated. "The fact that polio continues to occur is not due primarily to failure of the vaccine but failure to use it," he stressed. This was a dilemma that could not be solved in any lab, and it deeply troubled Jonas. But it also got him thinking about the need to approach human problems in new ways. Slowly an idea took shape in Salk's mind—a vision of his own future and that of medical research. In 1957 he shared his thoughts at a biology conference in New York. "The time is drawing to a close when one can hope to find full understanding of many more disease processes through one discipline alone," he said. He believed new breakthroughs would come when people from many fields had a chance to study problems together. For example, it took more than a vaccine to end the polio threat. It also required a knowledge of human behavior and politics. These were areas where psychologists, philosophers, and political scientists could help medical researchers.

The more Jonas thought about it, the more excited he became. In his early forties, he craved new challenges and broader horizons. "The world was open. Knowledge was expanding," Jonas said. "I wanted to be in the thick of things."

Often he thought back to the day that the results of his field test had been announced and to what his colleague Dr. Gregg had said to him. "Jonas, do only that which makes your heart leap."

Remembering that advice, Jonas imagined a setting—not a university, commercial company, or any traditional organization—but something totally different. In his mind's eye, Jonas saw an institute where leaders in many different fields shared their insights in common facilities. His heart leapt at the very thought. Salk knew that in his present position as professor of preventive medicine at the University of Pittsburgh there was no way to make his dream come true. Still, he couldn't let it go. He believed that people in such different disciplines as biology, chemistry, and philosophy had something to offer each other. His beliefs grew stronger as he talked with his friend Basil O'Connor.

Several years earlier, Jonas had remarked that he and O'Connor "understand each other as only a couple of crazy guys like us can." It was still true. O'Connor became just as excited as Jonas. What's more, he decided it was a perfect project to be supported by the National Foundation. O'Connor promised to provide funds for an independent research institute to be created by Jonas Salk.

For a whole year, Salk traveled the country with O'Connor, looking for the right place for his institute. He believed a peaceful, beautiful setting would promote creativity. Equally important, it would encourage scientists to think about how their work might change people's lives. During his travels, Salk heard of an architect named Louis Kahn who created strikingly original buildings and who had already designed research labs. In December 1959, Salk went to visit Kahn in Philadelphia. Armed with questions, Salk explained that he wanted the building itself to be a work of art, the kind of place "in which a Picasso would be comfortable working." Kahn's face lit up with immediate understanding. Salk knew he'd

Salk found in Louis Kahn, pictured here in 1972, the perfect architect for his institute.

found just the person to design his institute. But he still had to find a place to build it.

Earlier, Salk had visited La Jolla, a small community near San Diego in southern California. The breathtaking ocean views and dramatic brush-covered hillsides appealed to him. He was also excited because a branch of the University of California was being built in La Jolla. The new school offered possibilities to interact with other doctors and researchers.

In January 1960, one month after meeting Kahn, Salk flew back to California for a second look. He confided his hopes to city planning director Harry Haelsig, who promised to show him some sites. Since Jonas didn't want to be recognized while he made his tour, the two men disguised themselves by putting on their shabbiest clothes. Haelsig took Jonas to see the beautiful Torrey Pines mesa in La Jolla.

After wandering among the gnarled, sturdy pine trees and admiring the cliffs, Haelsig brought Jonas to some city parklands overlooking the Pacific Ocean. Standing above a deep canyon, Jonas gazed across the sparkling water to the horizon and said softly, "This is it." His long search was finally over.

Salk shows O'Connor a drawing of the site for his new institute.

ⓉⒺⓃ

Mad Enough to Fight
1960–1961

Although the mayor of San Diego wanted to donate the land for the institute, Jonas faced some disheartening problems. Many people in the small, exclusive community of La Jolla didn't want the institute near their homes. They felt the land should remain undeveloped, and they feared that laboratory animals might spread disease. They didn't say that Jonas was an outsider, but that's what some people were also thinking.

Jonas hoped that time would relieve their concerns as he quietly went ahead with his plans. Early in 1960, he brought Louis Kahn to see the proposed site and to figure out how much land would be needed for the buildings. That spring, the citizens of San Diego voted to donate 27 acres of land. At the insistence of Basil O'Connor and the city of San Diego, the research facility would be called the Salk Institute.

Salk began an exciting new adventure as he worked with Kahn to plan the buildings. Creating the institute was joyful, demanding, and time consuming. Jonas Salk loved every minute. But he also longed for more time in his lab back in Pittsburgh. "The reward for a job well done is the opportunity to do more," he often said. More than anything, Salk wanted to help create a world where everyone enjoyed good health. Cancer research was one of the areas of greatest need. Salk was beginning to explore the relationship between the immune system and tumor growth. Could something be done to help the immune system reject cancer, he wondered.

Meanwhile, the number of polio cases continued to decline as more children received shots. In 1960 only 3,190 people in the United States became ill with the disease. One year later, the number had fallen by almost one-third. The Salk vaccine had reduced the incidence of polio by over ninety-five percent from the epidemic proportions of 1950 to 1954. In spite of this, Albert Sabin was convinced that his way was best. Working feverishly, he developed an oral vaccine that contained weakened but live virus particles. As the weakened virus reproduced in the intestinal tract, it created a mild infection that did not harm the patient but still caused protective antibodies to form. Like the Salk vaccine before it, Sabin's oral vaccine would have to be tested for safety and effectiveness. But Sabin was forced to test his vaccine in Russia because the conquest of polio in the United States was almost complete.

The studies conducted in Russia lacked the precision of the National Foundation's double-blind field trial. But the rate of polio plummeted in areas where the Sabin vaccine was used. Grateful for the protection afforded their fellow citizens, Russian scientists supported Sabin at international polio conferences. Jonas found some of these conferences painful to attend. At one meeting, a prominent Russian researcher spoke against the Salk vaccine. It was difficult to kill all the virus particles, he said, and the Salk vaccine required injections.

Dr. Albert Sabin holds a vial of his live-virus vaccine.

The American medical establishment was also beginning to view the Sabin vaccine in a favorable light. Many doctors still believed that a live vaccine would induce the best immunity. Others liked the fact that the Sabin vaccine could be taken easily on a sugar cube. Politics and the Cold War may also have played a roll in swaying public opinion. This was a period of intense competition between the United States and Russia. The fact that Russia used a widely hailed oral vaccine alarmed some Americans. They were afraid the Russians might have a better vaccine than they did.

In June 1961, Jonas was in Atlantic City, New Jersey, where he was scheduled to give a speech. A newspaper headline caught his eye. The AMA was about to endorse Sabin's oral vaccine—even though it had not yet been licensed by the government. What do I do now, wondered a dismayed Jonas. Quickly buying the paper, Jonas read the AMA's recommendation that everyone—even persons already protected by the Salk vaccine—should be inoculated with Sabin's live-virus vaccine.

The last thing Jonas Salk wanted was a controversy. But the more he thought about the AMA's position, the more he knew that he couldn't keep silent. He realized that people might misunderstand his motives. They might think he was arguing to maintain his reputation as the conqueror of polio. It was a risk Jonas would have to take because an important scientific principle was at stake. If people who had received the Salk vaccine also took Sabin's live-virus vaccine, there would be no way to prove the long-term effectiveness of a killed-virus vaccine. Opponents could argue that antibodies in the blood had come from the Sabin and not the Salk vaccine.

Basil O'Connor noted a change in his friend. "This was the only time I have ever seen Jonas get mad enough and stay mad enough to fight back."

Salk wrote a detailed letter to the AMA disputing its statement that a live-virus vaccine might give longer lasting immunity than a killed-virus vaccine. He highlighted successes of the killed-virus approach that the AMA seemed to have overlooked. "Attention should be called to the virtual elimination of polio in Sweden and Denmark, as well as other countries, where killed-virus vaccine has been used," he said.

In spite of Salk's protests, the oral Sabin vaccine was licensed by the U.S. Public Health Service and soon replaced the killed-virus preparation. After mass immunizations began, however, an alarming situation emerged. Some people developed polio—not because the vaccine was incorrectly made but because of the nature of the vaccine itself. An investigation of several months revealed that the live-virus vaccine had caused dozens of cases of polio. Salk was deeply saddened. He had always feared that the weakened virus in the Sabin vaccine might revert to its virulent, disease-causing form. And since it was still alive, the virulent virus could be passed along to others, causing polio in individuals who had not been inoculated.

Since most of the vaccinated polio victims were adults, new guidelines advised people over eighteen not to take the live-virus vaccine. It was assumed that adults were more susceptible to the virus than children. But many youngsters who received the Sabin vaccine had previously been protected by the Salk vaccine. Since fewer adults had been immunized with the killed-virus vaccine, the adult population was, in fact, at greater risk of paralysis from the live-virus vaccine.

Jonas never understood why so many health officials supported the Sabin vaccine when the killed-virus vaccine had already come close to eliminating polio. Sometimes he thought it was almost a matter of chance or of timing. "If the live vaccine had been developed first, the killed vaccine would have been looked on as an improvement," he said.

It seemed that no amount of scientific data could convince Salk's opponents that a killed-virus vaccine was preferable. But then he had always known that some issues could not be solved in the lab. And that, after all, had been a crucial factor in his decision to found the Salk Institute.

Salk tours the Salk Institute for Biological Studies during construction.

ELEVEN

No Such Thing as Failure

1961–1995

All the while he defended the killed-virus vaccine, Jonas continued to plan the new institute. He could hardly wait to see the buildings rise on the California coastline. Shortly before construction was scheduled to start, Jonas met with Louis Kahn in La Jolla to sort through last-minute details. More than ever, Jonas loved the serenity and beauty of the spot he had chosen. But some doubts gnawed at the back of his mind. He had discussed them earlier with a colleague in Pittsburgh.

Early one evening, Jonas took a solitary walk around the site. Standing with his back to the ocean and the setting sun, Jonas tried to picture the four-building complex that he and Kahn had designed. But he had trouble imagining it. Yes, he realized, something was definitely wrong, though he couldn't quite put it into words.

Jonas had always trusted his intuition. After a restless night, he knew what he had to do. The next day, as he and Kahn flew to San Francisco to see Basil O'Connor, Jonas

103

explained his uneasiness. "I [think] we . . . have to start all over again," he said. Jonas thought the original plan was too cluttered. Whipping out a pad of paper, he drew a new plan for the institute.

Louis Kahn may have been surprised, but he wasn't afraid of hard work or starting over. He respected Jonas's instincts and understood his drive for perfection. After numerous meetings, he redesigned the complex according to Jonas's simpler scheme. Instead of four buildings, there were two identical structures flanking a wide courtyard.

Jonas was involved in all phases of construction. Every detail, from the texture of the concrete to the position of the pipes, fascinated him. In fact, he had a favorite saying, "God is in the details." Jonas Salk believed that nothing was unimportant. In a building or book, a painting or scientific theory, each detail added to the perfection of the whole.

During this hectic, exciting period Jonas also made several trips to Europe to recruit top scientists for the institute. But he still managed to spend several weeks each summer with his family at Deep Creek, Maryland.

In 1963 Jonas and his family moved to La Jolla, and the Salk Institute for Biological Studies opened in temporary quarters. Peter was in college and Darrell in boarding school by then, but during vacations they watched the progress on the institute.

Two years later, one of the permanent buildings was ready. Jonas and other scientists moved into the three-story lab building made of glass and concrete. Its mirror image across the rugged terrain was still an empty shell, but the two structures made the powerful architectural statement Salk had wanted. Office towers were angled so that each scientist's teakwood study had a spectacular ocean view.

Eventually a dazzling travertine courtyard, bisected by a small stream, would cover the ground between the buildings.

Jonas's hard work and planning had paid off. But as thrilled as he was to move into his new lab, he couldn't spend as much time as he wished on research. Administration and fund-raising claimed a great deal of his attention.

Jonas's long hours and public lifestyle, coupled with Donna's increasing community involvements placed a strain

The scientists' studies in the Salk Institute all have a view of the Pacific Ocean.

on their marriage. In 1968 Jonas and Donna were divorced.

Two years later at a dinner party, Jonas met Françoise Gilot, a painter, writer, and former companion of artist Pablo Picasso. Soon Jonas knew he had discovered someone special—someone with whom he shared a wide range of interests. After a brief courtship, Jonas and Françoise were married.

The couple settled in a modern house on a cliff in La Jolla. Every morning, Jonas rose around five o'clock, strolled out onto his patio, and gazed at the ocean. As the sun rose behind him, Jonas spoke his thoughts into a small tape recorder. He never tried to plan what he said. The flow of words that tumbled from his mind was "almost like sleepwalking," he

Jonas Salk and Françoise Gilot in 1970

explained. Later, in his study at the top of the house, he would organize his ideas. Jonas often ended his day by the ocean, too. He and Françoise liked to take long sunset walks along the beach.

Wherever he was, Jonas continued to ponder the human condition. Quiet, but passionate in his views, Jonas believed that humanity would conquer its social and ethical dilemmas as well as overcome illness and improve technology. He felt so strongly that he wrote several books to share his hopeful vision—*Man Unfolding,* published in 1972, was followed by *The Survival of the Wisest* one year later. In the early 1980s, he completed two more—*World Population and Human Values: A New Reality,* coauthored with his son Jonathan, and *Anatomy of Reality: Merging of Intuition and Reason.* In these writings, Jonas applied the principles of biology to human problems. Whether people were struggling with overpopulation, poverty, or war, there were lessons to be learned from nature. "I see good triumphing over evil as part of the process of evolution," he once said. But this kind of evolution didn't just happen—it depended on human creativity and cooperation. It also depended on education that brought out children's creative potential and sense of justice. "Can nobility be taught just as reading, writing, arithmetic, and biology are taught?" he asked in *Man Unfolding.*

Jonas believed it could. He invented the term "metabiology" to describe the way human culture and values fashion the future. Ideas were part of evolution as much as genes, he stressed. Men and women could use ideas consciously to shape a world in which cooperation was more important than competition. With this in mind, Jonas felt it was important for talented people to follow their vision freely. As a director of the charitable MacArthur Foundation, he helped identify imaginative individuals and award them grants to work in whatever field they wished.

People from all over the country continually called Jonas for advice. Even when he was interrupted at dinner or awakened at night, he was always ready to take the call. Whether in person or over the phone, Jonas warmly shared his thoughts, humor, and a deep-rooted faith in the future. "It was as if he was a vaccine in his own right," said his son Peter. "[Everyone] got a full dose."

Through the years, the people of San Diego came to value and respect the Salk Institute. Jonas became deeply involved in the community and enjoyed close relationships with his adult sons, all of whom became doctors. In 1972 Peter came to the institute to work with his father on cancer immunology. A very pleased Jonas took deep satisfaction in collaborating with Peter and in sharing his thoughts on evolution and the human mind with Jonathan.

Darrell was still in medical school in 1974 when he began discussing the merits of killed-virus versus live-virus vaccines with his father. Sabin's vaccine was still the only one used in the United States, although it caused several cases of polio each year. Jonas hadn't actively championed the killed-virus vaccine in a number of years. "Maybe it's time to do something again," Darrell suggested. "It's a new generation of medical students and physicians out there."

At first Jonas declined, but Darrell noticed a gleam of interest in his eyes. Eventually the two became coauthors of a review article that appeared in the journal *Science.* Jonas was tremendously proud of their partnership.

The publication marked Jonas's reentry into the vaccine controversy. He continued to write papers about polio with Darrell and went on to address government committees that

Jonas, center, *talks with San Diego residents Marion and Angelo Sammartino at the Salk Institute.*

made recommendations for childhood immunizations. And he cooperated with laboratories in France and the Netherlands to develop a stronger version of his killed-virus vaccine.

To make this more powerful vaccine, larger amounts of killed virus would be needed in each injection. The only question was how much. Jonas's work took him to Africa, where there were greater numbers of children who had not been immunized. Jonas designed studies to inoculate children with varying amounts of killed-virus vaccine. He reviewed the results of their blood tests to see how much antibody the different preparations had induced. Then he determined the dosage needed to confer full immunity with a single shot.

Jonas cared about how the vaccine was used as much as

how it was made. To improve health care, he suggested that the stronger polio vaccine be combined with the standard DPT shot in developing countries. Children would receive protection against diphtheria, whooping cough, tetanus, and polio all at once!

Past experience had taught Jonas that technology alone could not conquer disease. Politics, finances, and social issues all played a role in getting a vaccine to the people. Jonas and Darrell coined the term "vaccinology" to describe a scientific discipline that would encompass these broad roles. Vaccinology would include laboratory research as well as strategies to immunize whole populations. "There are scientific principles behind and beneath the way vaccines work," said Darrell Salk. "That's what [my father's] life was about."

Jonas was still deeply involved in the fight to eradicate polio worldwide when another disease began making headlines—acquired immunodeficiency syndrome (AIDS). In 1986, after attending a conference on AIDS in Paris, Jonas began to think seriously about this frightening condition that caused people's immune systems to break down.

Jonas knew that AIDS was triggered by the human immunodeficiency virus (HIV). The virus infected cells of the immune system and prevented the immune system from fighting viruses, bacteria, and other infections. A person with HIV developed AIDS after a long period of time. As the immune system gradually deteriorated, the person became more susceptible to a wide range of illnesses, from respiratory infections to cancer. Eventually patients would die from the inability to fight off disease.

Most researchers thought that once a person was infected with HIV, there was no way to prevent that person from getting sick with AIDS in several years. Salk refused to accept the patient's slow deterioration as inevitable. He believed it was possible to boost the immune systems of people who already had the virus so that they wouldn't develop the full disease of AIDS. While other researchers sought ways to prevent infection with HIV in the first place, Jonas began working on a vaccine for patients who were already infected. In addition to helping infected patients, he hoped his studies would lead to a vaccine for healthy people that would prevent AIDS entirely.

Once more, Salk was fighting for an idea unpopular with the medical establishment. "I know there are those waiting for failure," he remarked. "But my answer is that there is no such thing as failure. You can only fail if you stop too soon."

Jonas was in his mid-seventies, but he refused to let anything keep him down—even the infirmities of old age. Facing heart surgery in 1987, he looked forward to the renewed strength with which he could pursue his work.

That autumn, after Jonas had recoverd from the operation, twenty-five HIV-infected patients received his experimental vaccine. Some of them registered an increase in cellular immunity against the virus. Jonas was intrigued. Despite continued skepticism from the medical establishment, he kept right on working and conducting clinical trials. If only he asked the right questions, he believed he would find a way to beat AIDS. Soon other researchers began to take an interest in Salk's approach to an AIDS vaccine, and at Jonas's request, his son Peter joined him to help with the project.

On October 28, 1994, Jonas celebrated his eightieth birthday with hundreds of people at the Salk Institute. The next day, Peter and his eleven-year-old son, Michael, took Jonas to a local beach club for what they pretended would be a quiet brunch with Peter's wife, Ellen. Instead, Jonas found a room jammed with his sons, daughters-in-law, and grandsons—with cousins, nieces, and nephews. They had come from all over the country to wish him a happy birthday. A deeply moved Jonas surveyed the gathering from the youngest toddler to a face he had known since childhood. "You!" he exclaimed, pointing to Helen. Already he anticipated some good laughs.

Age and recurring health challenges hardly slowed Jonas down at all. Despite a hefty workload, he made time to visit Darrell's family in Seattle the next May. A visit from Grandpa was a great occasion to thirteen-year-old Jesse and nine-year-old Shane. "Would you like to visit my school?" an excited Shane asked. Shane's class was studying heroes. Jonas was

Jonas speaks with his grandson Shane and other children in Shane's third grade class.

tickled by the way Shane subtly "tricked" him into addressing the class on that topic.

Surrounded by second and third graders, Jonas relaxed and listened to them talk about heroes. This was the type of gathering he loved best. The youngsters were full of questions for their visiting hero, and Jonas gave each one his serious consideration. Then a child asked Jonas, "Who are your heroes?"

Jonas looked at the animated faces. "You are," he replied. "You are the hope. You are the future."

On June 23, 1995, Jonas Salk died of heart failure. Although he didn't live to see a victory over AIDS, his work gave new hope to many patients and their families. It continued to challenge other scientists to try new approaches. On hearing the news of his death, President Clinton called Jonas "a man who made this world a better place to live. His polio vaccine opened the door to a society in which good health is taken for granted."

Perhaps that's because Jonas Salk himself rarely took anything for granted. He asked hard questions, stubbornly pursued answers, and did things in his own way—just as he had always planned.

Afterword

On November 19, 1995, Jonas Salk was remembered and mourned at the dedication of an addition to the Salk Institute. The concrete and glass building seemed a fitting monument to Salk's far-sighted optimism and determination.

Some architects and members of the La Jolla community had fought the expansion of the institute. They argued that a new structure would weaken the power of the late Louis Kahn's buildings. But Jonas was used to facing opposition by then. He had overcome the critics who said a killed-virus vaccine would never work. He had won over a community that resisted his initial efforts to found a scientific institute in its midst. And he had pursued a unique line of AIDS research in the face of much skepticism.

Jonas had proven that a harmonious and striking addition to the Salk Institute was indeed possible. In the process, he had added many new labs to one of the nation's most respected research facilities. "I am constitutionally incapable of taking no for an answer," Jonas Salk often said.

For years, Salk had also continued to stress the merits of the killed-virus vaccine. Finally, in 2000, the U.S. Advisory

The Salk Institute for Biological Studies

Committee on Immunization Practices reconsidered his ideas. In a complete turnabout of previous policy, the committee decided to abandon the live-virus vaccine in favor of the Salk vaccine. The slight risk of polio inherent in the Sabin vaccine was deemed unacceptable in a nation where polio had essentially disappeared.

Jonas Salk's vision and tenacity are commemorated on a piece of travertine set in the main entryway of the Salk Institute. Engraved on the simple stone are his own words: "Hope lies in dreams, in imagination and in the courage of those who dare to make dreams into reality." Throughout the world, people reap the benefit of Jonas Salk's courage.

More about Polio

The full name of polio is poliomyelitis, a term that describes the inflammation of the gray matter (polios) in the spinal cord (myelos) of polio victims. The name was shortened to fit easily into newspaper stories.

It took researchers many years to figure out how polio is transmitted. House flies, garbage, car fumes, and foods such as ice cream and candy were just a few of the suspected culprits in the early 1900s. Today doctors know that polio probably spreads in two ways. In one instance, polio victims excrete the virus in their feces. The virus spreads when people don't wash their hands thoroughly after using the bathroom. Poliovirus enters the body through the mouth and multiplies in the digestive tract. From the intestines, the virus enters the bloodstream and travels to the nervous system where it causes paralysis. In the early infectious stages, polio can be passed along through coughing and sneezing in much the same way as viruses that cause the common cold.

Surprisingly, modern sanitation contributed to the rise of polio epidemics in the early twentieth century. Before the advent of a modern sewage system, most children were exposed to the poliovirus as infants. But they were protected by maternal antibodies that had passed to them through their mother's blood before birth. Because these antibodies kept the virus from entering the nervous system, the babies did not develop paralysis. Instead, a mild intestinal infection stimulated the creation of the infants' own antibodies. They grew up with a permanent immunity to polio.

As public hygiene—including modern plumbing and waste disposal—improved, most children weren't exposed to poliovirus while still protected by maternal antibodies. Thus, they had no chance to develop immunity. Later on, if they encountered the virus, they were at risk for severe consequences including paralysis and breathing difficulties.

The History of the National Foundation

In 1921 aspiring politician Franklin Roosevelt was stricken with polio at the age of thirty-nine. Five years later, determined to fight the severe paralysis in his legs, he purchased a run-down resort in Warm Springs, Georgia, where he had experienced some relief in the soothing pools. With the help of his law partner, Basil O'Connor, Roosevelt established a nonprofit organization, the Georgia Warm Springs Foundation, which became an international center for polio treatment.

When Roosevelt was elected president of the United States in 1932, he was in a unique position to help polio victims and to further research. Starting in 1934, a series of "Celebration Balls in Honor of the President's Birthday" was held all over the country. More than one million dollars were raised the first year—money that helped the Georgia Warm Springs Foundation care for an ever-growing number of patients. Finally, in 1937, Basil O'Connor persuaded Roosevelt to establish the National Foundation for Infantile Paralysis. Not only would the new organization fund therapy programs at Warm Springs, it would also support basic research to discover a way to prevent polio. (Fittingly, the announcement in Ann Arbor of the Salk vaccine's success came on the tenth anniversary of Franklin Roosevelt's death.)

As actors and actresses became more active in fund-raising for the National Foundation, radio personality Eddie Cantor had an idea to get more people involved. He suggested that appeals for money be made during popular radio programs. In the

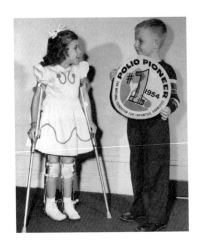

The 1955 March of Dimes poster child, Mary Kosloski, meets the first Polio Pioneer, Randy Kerr. They represented the National Foundation's double aims of polio treatment and prevention.

late 1930s, a regular feature at the movies was a newsreel known as the "March of Time." Playing on the name, Cantor dubbed his radio campaign the "March of Dimes" and asked everyone listening to mail a dime to the White House. Within days, the White House was flooded with over 200,000 letters. The man in charge of the postal service at the White House faced an almost impossible challenge. "The government of the United States darned near stopped functioning because we couldn't clear away enough dimes to find the official White House mail," he grumbled. To keep the White House running smoothly, people were soon asked to donate their dimes at their local movie theater instead of through the mail.

The End of Polio?

In 1988 the World Health Organization (WHO) set a goal of worldwide eradication of polio. By the end of 2000, the global incidence of polio had dropped by ninety-nine percent since the onset of the WHO campaign. Despite this encouraging statistic, people are still contracting polio, mainly in South Asia and sub-Saharan Africa. Extensive vaccination campaigns with the live-virus vaccine are under way to reach children in the hardest hit areas.

Before polio can be considered eliminated, health officials must investigate an area for three to five years without finding any documented cases of the disease. If and when that happens, the naturally occurring "wild-type" poliovirus would continue to exist only in carefully safeguarded laboratories. Some officials of the WHO believe that there would then no longer be any need for polio immunizations.

Some scientists have questioned, however, whether polio can ever be completely eliminated as long as the live-virus vaccine is used. Since the weakened poliovirus in the vaccine can sometimes revert to a virulent, disease-causing form, dangerous vaccine-derived poliovirus could continue to spread disease.

This suspicion has been confirmed by recent findings. In Japan, where naturally occurring poliovirus has been eliminated, virulent poliovirus was identified in sewage and river water. Laboratory analysis revealed that the virus had come from the live vaccine and had mutated back to a virulent form. In the Dominican Republic and Haiti, an outbreak of 49 confirmed and suspected polio cases was traced to the live-virus vaccine. A strain of virus from the vaccine apparently reverted to its virulent form. This dangerous virus was then passed on from person to person, circulating in the communities until some people contracted paralytic polio.

The U.S. Advisory Committee on Immunization Practices recently changed its policy and now recommends the exclusive use of the Salk vaccine in order to avoid cases of vaccine-associated polio in the United States, where circulating wild-type poliovirus is no longer a cause of disease. Some scientists believe that a similar change will need to be made throughout the world in order to get rid of the last vestiges of the virus.

Sources

p. 12   *Marching to a Different Drummer: The Life and Career of Jonas Salk,* Carolina Video, 1991, Videocassette.

p. 13   Greer Williams, *Virus Hunters* (New York: Knopf, 1959), 272.

p. 13   Helen Glickstein (cousin of Jonas Salk), telephone interview by author, 25 August 1998.

p. 14   Richard Carter, *Breakthrough: The Saga of Jonas Salk* (New York: Trident, 1966), 30.

p. 17   Williams, *Virus Hunters,* 273.

p. 22   Jonas Salk, "The Creative Mind," interview by Joan Rachel Goldberg, *Science Digest,* June 1984, 51.

p. 22   Peter Salk, telephone interview by author, 31 August 2000.

p. 24   Williams, *Virus Hunters,* 278.

p. 26   Carter, *Breakthrough,* 38.

p. 26   Ibid.

p. 27   Williams, *Virus Hunters,* 279.

p. 29   Carter, *Breakthrough,* 51.

p. 30   Peter Salk, telephone interview by author, 14 January 2001.

p. 31   Carter, *Breakthrough,* 48.

p. 34   Ibid., 53.

p. 34   Ibid., 5.

p. 37   Ibid., 62.

p. 40   Ibid., 83.

p. 41   Ibid., 81.

p. 42   Ibid., 82.

p. 50   Ibid., 108.

p. 51   Ibid., 95–6.

p. 51   Carter, *Breakthrough,* 130. Also "Closing in on Polio," *Time,* 29 March 1954, 62.

p. 52   Carter, *Breakthrough,* 106.

p. 53   Williams, *Virus Hunters,* 286.

p. 59   Carter, *Breakthrough,* 138.

p. 61   Ibid., 140.

p. 64   Tony Gould, *A Summer's Plague: Polio and Its Survivors* (New Haven: Yale University Press, 1955), 136. Also Jane S. Smith, *Patenting the Sun: Polio and the Salk Vaccine* (New York: Anchor Books, 1990), 186.

p. 64   Smith, *Patenting the Sun,* 187.

p. 65   Helen Glickstein, telephone interview by author, 10 August 1998.

p. 67   Carter, *Breakthrough,* 173.

p. 72   Ibid., 166.

p. 72   Ibid., 214–5.

p. 72   Ibid., 215.

p. 74   Robert Coughlan, "Tracking the Killer," *Life,* 22 February 1954.

p. 75   Carter, *Breakthrough,* 231; Smith, *Patenting the Sun,* 258.

p. 75   Dorothy Ducas, "Jonas Salk," in *Heroes for Our Times,* eds. Will Yolen and Kenneth Giniger (Harrisburg, PA: Stackpole Books, 1968), 80.

p. 77   Transcript of radio broadcast, "The Scientist Speaks for Himself," April 26, 1954.

p. 81   Smith, *Patenting the Sun,* 326.

p. 81   Carter, *Breakthrough,* 285.

p. 81   Ibid., 274.

p. 82   Ibid.

p. 82   Carter, *Breakthrough,* 284. Also Smith, *Patenting the Sun,* 338.

p. 84   Donna Salk, telephone interview by author, 19 January 2001.

p. 84   Carter, *Breakthrough,* 289.

p. 84   Ibid.

p. 84   Ibid., 292.

p. 86   Carter, *Breakthrough,* 295–6. Also Smith, *Patenting the Sun,* 358.

p. 88   Carter, *Breakthrough,* 331.

p. 92 Carter, *Breakthrough,* 350. Also
John Troan, *Passport to
Adventure: Or, How a Typewriter
from Santa Led to an Exciting
Lifetime Journey.* (Pittsburgh:
Neworks Press, 2000), 234.

p. 92 Carter, *Breakthrough,* 370.

p. 92 Ibid., 405.

p. 93 Ibid., 274.

p. 93 Ibid., 274.

p. 93 Ibid., 173.

p. 94 Jonas Salk, "Horizons into the
Future," *Arts & Antiques,*
December 1990, 10.

p. 95 Neil Morgan, "Saluting the New
Salk and Recalling the Old," *San
Diego Union-Tribune,*
14 November 1995.

p. 98 Christine Kindl, "The Creation of
a Cure," *Focus Magazine* of the
Greenburg Tribune Review,
9 September 1990, 8.

p. 100 Carter, *Breakthrough,* 375.

p. 100 Ibid., 378.

p. 101 Peter Salk, telephone interview by
author, 25 July 1996.

p. 104 Jonas Salk, "Horizons into the
Future," 10.

p. 104 Peter Salk, telephone interview by
author, 25 July 1996.

p. 107 *Marching to a Different Drummer.*

p. 107 Jonas Salk, *Man Unfolding* (New
York: Harper & Row, 1972), 93.

p. 108 Peter Salk, telephone interview
by author, 25 July 1996.

p. 108 Darrell Salk, telephone
interview by author, 19 January
2001.

p. 110 Ibid.

p. 111 Sheryl Stolberg, "Jonas Salk,
Whose Vaccine Conquered
Polio, Dies at 80," *Los Angeles
Times,* 24 June 1995.

p. 112 Peter Salk, telephone interview
by author, 15 January 2001.

p. 112 Darrell Salk, telephone
interview by author, 19 January
2001.

p. 113 Ibid.

p. 113 Jack Williams, "Jonas Salk,
Father of the Polio Vaccine Dead
at 80," *San Diego Union-Tribune,*
24 June 1995.

p. 114 Cheryl Clark, "Stubborn Streak
was Salk Hallmark," *San Diego
Union-Tribune,* 25 June 1995.
Also Peter Salk, telephone
interview by author, 15 January
2001.

p. 115 The Family of Jonas Salk and
the Jonas Salk Trust.

p. 118 Smith, *Patenting the Sun,* 74.

Selected Bibliography

Works by Jonas Salk

Anatomy of Reality: Merging of Intuition and Reason. New York: Columbia University Press, 1983.

"The Creative Mind: Jonas Salk." Interview by Joan Rachel Goldberg. *Science Digest,* June 1984.

"An Evolutionary Philosophy for Our Time." In *Living Philosophies: The Reflections of Some Eminent Men and Women of Our Time.* Edited by Clifton Fadiman. New York: Doubleday, 1990.

"Horizons into the Future." *Arts and Antiques,* December 1990.

Man Unfolding. New York: Harper and Row, 1972.

"Preconceptions about Vaccination against Poliomyelitis." *Annals of Internal Medicine,* 50, no. 4 (April 1959).

The Survival of the Wisest. New York: Harper and Row, 1973.

With G. I. Lavin and Thomas Francis, Jr., M.D. "The Antigenic Potency of Epidemic Influenza Virus Following Inactivation by Ultraviolet Radiation." *Journal of Experimental Medicine* 72, no. 6 (December 1940).

With Darrell Salk. "Control of Influenza and Poliomyelitis with Killed Virus Vaccines." *Science* 195 (March 1977).

With Darrell Salk. "Vaccinology of Poliomyelitis." *Vaccine,* 2 (March 1984).

With Jonathan Salk. *World Population and Human Values: A New Reality.* New York: Harper and Row, 1981.

With Peter L. Salk. "An Evolutionary Approach to World Problems." *World Affairs,* 1 (January 1990).

Books

Black, Kathryn. *In the Shadow of Polio: A Personal and Social History.* Reading, MA: Addison-Wesley, 1996.

Carter, Richard. *Breakthrough: The Saga of Jonas Salk.* New York: Trident, 1966.

Dowling, Harry F. *Fighting Infection: Conquests of the Twentieth Century.* Cambridge: Harvard University Press, 1977.

Ducas, Dorothy. "Jonas Salk." In *Heroes for Our Times,* edited by Will Yolen and Kenneth Seeman Giniger. Harrisburg, PA: Stackpole Books, 1968.

Gould, Tony. *A Summer's Plague: Polio and its Survivors.* New Haven: Yale University Press, 1995.

Klein, Aaron E. *Trial by Fury: The Polio Vaccine Controversy.* New York: Charles Scribner's Sons, 1972.

Moyers, Bill. *A World of Ideas.* New York: Doubleday, 1989.

Paul, John R. *A History of Poliomyelitis.* New Haven: Yale University Press, 1971.

Smith, Jane S. *Patenting the Sun: Polio and the Salk Vaccine.* New York: Doubleday, 1990.

Steele, James. *Salk Institute: Louis I. Kahn.* London: Phaidon, 1993.

Troan, John. *Passport to Adventure: Or, How a Typewriter from Santa Led to an Exciting Lifetime Journey.* Pittsburgh: Neworks Press, 2000.

Williams, Greer. *Virus Hunters.* New York: Knopf, 1959.

Newspapers and Periodicals

Brown, David. "Each Child a Step in WHO's Plan To Erase Polio." *Washington Post,* 2 October 2000.

Clark, Cheryl. "Stubborn Streak was Salk Hallmark." *San Diego Union-Tribune,* 25 June 1995.

"Closing in on Polio." *Time,* 29 March 1954.

Coughlan, Robert. "Tracking the Killer." *Life,* 22 February 1954.

Greenfelder, Leise. "Polio Outbreak Raises Questions about Vaccine." *Science,* 8 December 2000.

Kindl, Christine. "The Creation of a Cure." *Focus Magazine, Greensburg Tribune Review,* 9 September 1990.

Morgan, Neil. "Salk's Towering Role in a Modern San Diego." *San Diego Union-Tribune,* 25 June 1995.

———. "Saluting the New Salk and Recalling the Old." *San Diego Union-Tribune,* 14 November 1995.

"A Quiet Young Man's Magnificent Victory." *Newsweek,* 15 April 1955.

Stolberg, Sheryl. "Jonas Salk, Whose Vaccine Conquered Polio, Dies at 80." *Los Angeles Times,* 24 June 1995.

Williams, Jack. "Jonas Salk, Father of Polio Vaccine Dead at 80." *San Diego Union-Tribune,* 24 June 1995.

Interviews

Glickstein, Helen. Telephone conversations with author, 10, 25 August 1998.

Salk, Darrell. Telephone conversations with author, 18, 19 January 2001.

Salk, Donna. Telephone conversation with author, 19 January 2001.

Salk, Peter. Telephone conversations with author, 25 July 1996; 29 August 1996; 31 August 2000; 14, 15, 16, 31 January 2001.

Videos and Exhibits

Bronowski, Judith. *Jonas Salk: Personally Speaking.* San Diego, KPBS, 1998. Videocassette.

Marching to a Different Drummer: The Life and Career of Jonas Salk. Burlington, North Carolina, and Gladstone, Oregon: Carolina Video, 1991. Videocassette.

"The Shot Heard 'Round the World: The Development of the Salk Polio Vaccine 1947–1955." Text of exhibit located at the University of Pittsburgh, School of Pharmacy, Salk Hall.

Websites

Global Polio Eradication Initiative of the World Health Organization (WHO)
    <http://www.polioeradication.org>
March of Dimes Archive
    <http://www.modimes.org/About2/Archives>
National Immunization Program of the Centers for Disease Control (CDC)
    <http://www.cdc.gov/nip/global>
Salk Polio Vaccine Commemoration at the Historical Center for the Health Sciences at the University of Michigan
    <http://www.med.umich.edu/HCHS/articles/PolioExhibit>
World Health Organization (WHO)
    <http://www.who.int>
A World without Polio from the United Nations Children's Education Fund (UNICEF)
    <http://www.unicef.org/polio>

Author's Acknowledgments

I would like to express my deepest thanks and appreciation to Peter Salk and Darrell Salk for generously sharing their time, memories, and anecdotes. Our long conversations greatly enriched my understanding of their father. In addition, their scientific explanations and materials helped strengthen the technical aspects of this book. Any errors are, of course, my own.

A special thank you to Donna Salk for sharing recollections of the vaccine's development and the announcement of its success. Her words made events more vivid to me.

Thanks also to Helen Glickstein for sharing memories of her cousin's childhood; to Helen Deitch for her remembrances of Jonas Salk's early years; to Ann Roberti, Earl Walls, Jack MacAllister, and Ruth Haelsig for discussing details about the Salk Institute; and to Adele Simmons for her information on Salk's work with the MacArthur Foundation.

Finally, thanks to my editor Susan Rose for her support and insights and to my husband, Richard, and daughters Jennifer and Marianne for their enthusiasm and suggestions.

Index

New York University's College of Medicine, 17, 19, 20-22, 24
Nix, Robert, 65

O'Connor, Basil, 54–55, 64, 67, 72, 77, 80, 90, 93–94, 96, 97, 100, 103–104, 117
oral vaccine. *See* live-virus vaccine, Sabin vaccine

placebo, 69, 77
polio (poliomyelitis), 9, 35–36, 48, 49–51, 57, 86, 108, 116–117; epidemics, 10, 48, 49, 62, 69, 116; patients, 35–36, 48, 49–50, 55, 57–59, 70, 117, 118; spread of, 9–10, 116–117
Polio Pioneers, 76, 77, 78, 118
polio vaccines, 20, 47, 69. *See also* killed-virus vaccine, live-virus vaccine, Sabin vaccine, Salk vaccine
polio vaccine trials, 57–59, 61–62, 65–67, 98–99. *See also* field trial of polio vaccine
poliovirus, 20, 53, 61, 74, 87, 119; production in laboratory, 43–47, 52; strains of, 52; types of, 36–37, 41, 52, 80; typing project, 36–47
presidential citations, 85, 115
Press, Helen (cousin), 13, 20, 65–66, 112
publicity, 57, 64–65, 71–72, 80–84, 91

research methods, 20–21, 30–31, 41, 43–45, 52, 59, 61, 67
Roosevelt, Franklin, 117

Sabin, Albert, 41, 54, 62–63, 74–75, 88, 98, 99
Sabin vaccine, 98–101, 115
Salk, Daniel (father), 8, 9–10, 14, 15, 16, 19

Salk, Darrell (son), 6–7, 32–33, 34, 40, 78, 79, 83, 84, 104, 108, 110, 112
Salk, Donna (wife), 22–26, 28, 29, 32-33, 34, 40–41, 51, 61–62, 65, 71, 78, 79, 83, 84, 105–106
Salk, Dora (mother), 8, 9–10, 12, 14, 15, 17, 19, 28
Salk, Herman (brother), 12–14, 15, 28
Salk, Jesse (grandson), 112
Salk, Jonas: childhood, 9–16; education, 13–27; ethics of, 12–13, 14–15, 49, 56, 69–71, 82, 86, 113; family life, 25, 26, 29, 34, 40–41, 51, 65, 71, 92, 104, 111–112; independence of, 13, 14, 27, 32, 42, 47, 108–109, 113; intuition of, 7, 22, 25, 29–30, 56, 91, 92–93, 103–104, 106–107; kindness of, 7, 13, 25–26, 39–40, 55, 57–59, 108; writings, 21, 64, 107, 108, 122
Salk, Jonathan (son), 51, 65, 78, 79, 83, 84, 107, 108
Salk, Lee (brother), 14, 15, 28
Salk, Michael (grandson), 111
Salk, Peter (son), 32–33, 34, 40–41, 42, 78, 79, 83, 84, 104, 108, 111
Salk, Shane (grandson), 112–113
Salk Institute, 93–95, 96, 97, 102, 103–105, 108, 114–115
Salk vaccine, 64, 68, 72–75, 80–81, 87–89, 91, 113, 115; effectiveness of, 80–81, 98, 100–101, 119
Sammartino, Angelo and Marion, 109

University of Michigan, 27, 29–30, 80
University of Pittsburgh, 33–35, 45, 93

Photo Acknowledgments

Photographs have been reproduced with the permission of: The Family of
Jonas Salk and the Jonas Salk Trust, pp. 1, 8, 12, 15, 18, 23, 28, 33, 79, 83;
Archive Photos, pp. 2, 38, 40, 46, 60, 63, 66, 82, 99; Brown Brothers, pp. 11, 68;
AP/Wide World Photos, pp. 30, 48, 55, 76, 80, 90, 102; © Bettmann/CORBIS,
pp. 35, 43, 44, 53, 73, 85, 88, 89, 94, 96, 106, 118; Library of Congress, p. 36;
The Nobel Foundation, p. 45; © Josef Scaylea/CORBIS, p. 50; *Minneapolis
Times*/The Minneapolis Public Library, p. 58; © Hulton-Deutsch Collection/
CORBIS, p. 70; Stephanie McPherson, pp. 87, 109; © G.E. Kidder-Smith/
CORBIS, pp. 105, 115; The Family of Jonas Salk and the Jonas Salk
Trust/Photo by Lindsay Horton, p. 112.

Cover photo courtesy of Archive Photos.